THE SOURCE OF SILENCE

JOURNEY INWARD TO THE TRUE SELF

SIRSHREE

The Source of Silence
By **Sirshree** Tejparkhi

Copyright © Tejgyan Global Foundation
All Rights Reserved 2020

Tejgyan Global Foundation is a charitable organization
with its headquarters in Pune, India.

ISBN : 978-81-8415-721-5

Published by WOW Publishings Pvt. Ltd., India

First edition published in December 2020

Printed and bound by Trinity Academy, Pune, INDIA

Based on the Hindi book titled "Moun Niyam" by Sirshree Tejparkhi

Copyrights are reserved with Tejgyan Global Foundation and publishing rights are vested exclusively with WOW Publishings Pvt. Ltd. This book is sold subject to the condition that it shall not by way of trade or otherwise, be lent, resold, hired out, or otherwise circulated without the publisher's prior written consent in any form of binding or cover other than that in which it is published and without a similar condition including this condition being imposed on the subsequent purchaser and without limiting the rights under copyright reserved above, no part of this publication may be reproduced, stored in or introduced into a retrieval system, or transmitted, in any form, or by any means, electronic, mechanical, photocopying, recording or otherwise, without the prior written permission of both the copyright owner and the above-mentioned publisher of this book. Any person who does any unauthorized act in relation to this publication may be liable to criminal prosecution and civil claims for damages.

Although the author and publisher have made every effort to ensure accuracy of content in this book, they hereby disclaim any liability to any party for any loss, damage, or disruption caused by errors or omissions, resulting from negligence, accident, or any other cause. Readers are advised to take full responsibility to exercise discretion in understanding and applying the content of this book.

To
The Eternal Silence
that is present before the world comes into existence,
that is present now,
and is present even after the world has ceased to exist.

How to fully benefit from this book

1. Please read the book from start to end in the given sequence.
2. At places in the chapters where you find the notation "………", take a pause, reflect, and be in silence.
3. If you are unable to understand any of the sentences, park them aside, and continue reading further. They will eventually become clear by the time you finish reading the entire book.
4. Every chapter reveals a unique nuance of Silence. With superficial reading, the content may seem repetitive, but deep reading will reveal new aspects
5. It will be helpful to read each chapter again as every reading can give new insights.

Contents

	Preface	7
PART 1 - RECOGNIZING SILENCE		**13**
1.	How to Enter the State of Silence	15
2.	Letting Silence Unfold	19
3.	Tasting the Wordless Essence of Silence	25
PART 2 - OBSTACLES IN REACHING SILENCE		**33**
4.	The Two Possibilities of Thoughts	35
5.	Frozen Thoughts	37
6.	Recorded Thinking of the Past	43
7.	Past Happiness and Past Sorrow	48
8.	The Notion of Doer-ship	52
PART 3 - THE TRAPS OF THE MIND		**57**
9.	The Web of Emotions	59
10.	The Stories of the Mind	64
11.	The Trap of Attachment	69
12.	Demonic Tendencies	74

13.	The Stages of True Detachment	77
14.	The Maze of Desires	84

PART 4 - AWAKENING OF THE REAL I — 87

15.	The Real Character in the Present	89
16.	Attacking the Root Belief	97
17.	The Real I and the False I's	101
18.	Walking with Faith on the Highway to Silence	108
19.	The Wondrous Game of the Self	112
20.	Knowing without a Knower	118

PART 5 - HOW TO EXPERIENCE SILENCE — 123

21.	The Sense of Beingness	125
22.	Zero is Positive	131
23.	Self-Experience with Right Understanding	135
24.	The State of Complete Surrender	140
25.	The Joy of Surrendering with Understanding	145
26.	The Art of Complete Surrender	148
27.	Being the Harmonium	152
28.	The Practice of Samadhi	156
29.	The Practice of Abiding in the Self	160
30.	The Glory of Words Leading to Silence	164

PREFACE

To live without being aware of
Silence is like sleepwalking

Once, a monk was passing by a kingdom. Whatever he preached on his way shook the beliefs of those who listened to him. Some couldn't accept what he preached. Some considered him insane and ignored his words. Others felt compelled to reflect on his words. Several questions arose in their minds that challenged all the concepts and ideas they had grown to believe since their childhood.

Some orthodox people were troubled and furious at his words. They feared that people would get influenced by him and start disregarding the prevalent social beliefs. They approached the king and complained, "O King! A mad monk is roaming the streets and misguiding our people."

The king ordered that the so-called madman be taken into custody and summoned to his court. When the monk arrived in the royal court, the king fired a volley of questions—

"Who has permitted you to challenge our beliefs and customs? Who are you? Are you a scholar?"

"I am beyond that," replied the monk.

The king asked him, "Are you a Guru?"

"Beyond that."

The king was enraged.

"Oh... so then are you God?!"

"Beyond that."

"But there is nothing beyond God."

"I am that Nothing."

"I didn't understand."

After being in silence for some time, the monk replied, "It is simple. There is nothing mysterious about what I say. I only talk about that which transcends your beliefs and concepts. Whatever you consider me—a monk, a saint, a guru, a scholar, and so on—they are mere words. They are your preconceived notions that appear as thoughts. I speak of the experience of Silence, the experience of beingness, the experience of pure consciousness."

The king was perplexed, "I didn't understand what you just said. Can you elaborate?"

"Words cannot describe this experience; they can only point at it. When words do not serve to throw light on this experience, they lose their significance and mislead us from the Truth. It then becomes necessary to uproot these ideas and beliefs to awaken pure consciousness. I spoke to your people considering this possibility. The pure experience that I speak of is beyond words, beyond all religious dogma."

The king could not comprehend anything, but he could sense a conviction of truth in the monk's words. His demeanor tempered down. Politely he said, "O revered master, I find it difficult to understand this experience. Kindly narrate this experience in one line for our sake so that we all can grasp it."

"Let me give you a word," said the monk and immediately became silent.

With folded hands, the king requested, "O Saint! What is that word?"

The monk closed his eyes. With sheer peace emanating from his radiant face, he calmly uttered, "Silence" and again became silent………………...……………………...……

……………………………………………….............………………

After a few moments of silence, the king exclaimed in wonder, "How can one attain this Silence?"

"In meditation," replied the monk.

The king asked, "And how can one meditate?"

The monk smiled, "By being in Silence."……………...

………………………………………………….............…………

What the monk told the king is not just a play of words, but a pointer to the ultimate truth.

Silence is the source of all that is. This entire world emerges from Silence, from the Nothing that is teeming with infinite possibilities. Of all living beings, only humans can reflect on this Silence and realize it. However, this is possible only when human life attains the second birth.

Man is born the first time when he emerges from the mother's womb. He experiences freedom from the confines of the womb and arrives in the bigger world. However, he does not realize that he has only shifted from the mother's womb into the womb of this illusory world.

When he breaks out of the web of all beliefs and concepts borrowed from the world and experiences his true nature in Silence, he becomes free from the womb of this illusory world and attains the second birth.

It is only after this second birth that Silence begins to express itself in our life. Thereafter, we lead our life by abiding in that experience. It is then that we start living in a true sense. Hence, the second birth can also be known as the highest way of living.

This book takes us through three important steps to realize Silence:

- At the first step, we will try to understand Silence. As the monk mentioned, words cannot describe it. But words can, at best, be used to point at it. We need to sense what these words point at without getting attached to them.

- At the second step, we will understand the obstacles in experiencing Silence and how to overcome them.

- At the third step, we will prepare ourselves to dive deep into the experience of Silence.

We all, without exception, have experienced Silence—from the moment we were born till we were about two to three years old. But as we grew up, we have lost this experience due to beliefs and concepts borrowed from the world.

Some of us have got glimpses of this experience even after growing up, but we have unknowingly lost it due to a lack of recognition of what it truly is. However, some have experienced this Silence and stabilized in it. We refer to them as Self-realized souls.

It is now time to understand what Silence is, experience it, and be established in it. This book serves as a definitive source to understand Silence, journey towards the experience, and abide in it.

Let's begin this auspicious journey with a prayer—

> **Starting from today, let my life be an expression of the blooming presence of Silence.**

PART 1
RECOGNIZING SILENCE

We function in our life in three dimensions: body, *prana*, and mind.

In the body's dimension, we make progress through physical exercises and the right diet to boost our physical health.

In the *pranic* dimension, we progress by practicing pranayama to regulate our breathing so that the vital force replenishes and rejuvenates the body efficiently.

The dimension of the mind operates at the level of thoughts and feelings. We progress in this dimension by understanding the laws of thought and aligning our thoughts and feelings in the direction of our life purpose. By understanding how our thoughts and feelings are seeds that we sow for our future, we work upon enriching their quality.

However, there also exists a fourth dimension, which very few people know. It is the source of these three. This is the dimension of Silence—the very foundation whence all the three dimensions emerge, and it transcends them all. Literally speaking, we cannot call it a "dimension", as it transcends all dimensions. The body and mind have no direct role to play in it. Life attains completeness only when we revel in this experience of Silence.

Silence is the invisible essence of our life, the backdrop of everything, the source of true happiness. It is like an ever-blooming lotus, waiting to be unraveled petal by petal. When this lotus of Silence blossoms totally, our life becomes complete with true love, bliss, and peace.

1

How to Enter the State of Silence

A king had four sons. He was in a dilemma about choosing the heir to his throne. He then approached his guru to seek advice. The guru assured him, "Give me a year. I would like to have four palaces built. Then we can resolve this matter easily." The king agreed.

True to his promise, the guru got four palaces built by the end of the year. He called upon the king and instructed, "Entrust each of your sons with one palace and one hundred gold coins each. Tell them that whoever spends the coins most effectively to fill his palace in the best possible way will be the heir to your throne."

Now, each of the princes got busy decorating their respective palaces.

The first prince filled his palace with plenty of worn-out furniture bought from the re-sale market.

The second prince gambled away the money, only to win some more. He bought new elegant modern furniture with that money and decorated his palace.

The third prince thought differently. He bought lots of flowers from the market and filled his palace with their fragrance.

After visiting these three palaces, the king and the guru proceeded to the fourth palace. The fourth prince requested them, "Your Majesty and Revered master! May I enter the palace first? Can you all please enter after some time and witness what happens?" An enigmatic smile appeared on the guru's lips.

The prince entered the palace. After some time, when the king and the guru entered the palace, it was pitch dark. Then all of a sudden, the palace shone bright with white light. The awestruck king looked at the prince in amazement. He was sitting at a place whence the light was radiating.

The king inquired, "What is the secret of this brilliant light?"

The prince narrated, "When I entered the palace for the first time, I thoroughly examined it. I found this mysterious space right here. I wondered what its use and purpose could be. It struck me that there was surely some secret behind it, and I felt the need to investigate it.

"I saw a black curtain covering the wall, although there was no window behind it. Its color wasn't matching the color of the wall.

"I thought that there must be a secret hidden behind this curtain. As I unveiled the curtain, I found some more curtains behind it. After unveiling all of them, I spotted a brick in the wall. Removal of the brick revealed a hidden message behind it, 'Be seated in silence here and see what happens!'

"I immediately sat in silence out of curiosity. In some time, white light radiated all over the place, and the entire palace was illuminated. I felt, 'What can be better than this divine light that can fill the palace!'"

You might be wondering whether that place was kept only in the fourth palace. No! The guru had built this place in all the four palaces. But only the fourth prince could discover it. He first examined the palace, decoded the clue, and assessed it. He could discern the truth.

The fourth prince returned the unused hundred coins to the guru and said, "I didn't use them earlier, nor will I use them later. I have experienced the bliss of Silence. I feel contented."

The guru told the king, "Here is your rightful heir!"

Let us now understand the hidden pointers in this story. The palace represents our body-mind mechanism. We have been blessed with this wondrous body-mind to experience the bliss of Silence and express it to the fullest, like a full-bloomed lotus flower. The curtains that the prince unveiled represent the three dimensions of body, *prana* and mind that need to be transcended to enter Silence.

The place discovered by the fourth prince is the "Seat of Silence." One, who decodes the pointers of life and discerns the truth, discovers this seat of Silence. ....
....

We, too, need to find the seat of Silence within ourselves and stay on it. Most people fail to reach this place as they are unaware of it. Even if they are aware of it, they lack the motivation to go beyond the three dimensions and stay in Silence.

Why was the fourth prince chosen as the rightful heir to the throne? It is because the one who has experienced the bliss of Silence has essentially attained everything. He alone can guide others in the right direction. Only those who seek inspiration from Silence within, can truly inspire the world.

This metaphorical story emphasizes the importance of discovering the Silence within us. It is essential to become pure and empty before diving deep into the utter stillness of Silence.

In the further chapters of this book, we will understand what we can attain by dwelling in Silence. We will develop the inner eye to discern Silence, abiding in which the fourth prince felt contented and became the rightful heir to the kingdom of divinity.

Questions for Contemplation

- Do you feel inspired to explore the seat of Silence? Do you wish to abide in the experience of Silence?
- Are you investing time to let the lotus of Silence blossom to the fullest?
- What is the difference between being in Silence and the feeling of boredom?

2

Letting Silence Unfold

Silence is the source of life. It is the unmanifested source of all existence. It is the origin of the manifested world. We cannot describe it in words. It has been given different names in spirituality such as Divinity, "I Am That," "*Sat Chit Anand*," "Universal Self," "Pure Consciousness," "Beingness," "Absolute Truth," and so on.

Silence is beyond thinking. It is pure beingness that revels in its own existence. We can experience it by only being in the stillness of inner silence. When thoughts arise, we experience the noise of the content of thoughts. When thoughts subside, we feel an inner tranquility due to the absence of thoughts. But Silence is beyond both noise and tranquility. It is the source of both noise and tranquility.

In this book, we will refer to it as **Silence** with an upper-case 'S.' It is important to bear in mind that Silence is the background of both noise and tranquility (the absence of noise). Noise and silence, both, are experienced in this Silence.

The three dimensions of life viz. body, *prana*, and thoughts, arise and subside in this Silence. Hence, it can also be called the fourth dimension or *Turiya*. Silence is experienced as the awareness of existence, as the presence in which everything unfolds. It is the experience of the true Self. Our true Self is realized in Silence.

The unfolding of Silence

The ultimate purpose of human life is to experience Silence and allow it to manifest to the fullest. When Silence manifests to the fullest in our life, we reach our highest evolved state. We need to empty ourselves from within and become like a flute for the divine tune of Silence to play through us.

There are numerous examples of artists who have brilliantly expressed their art, created masterpieces, and mesmerized audiences. Yet, they have not taken any credit for their masterstrokes. They honestly admit, "I don't know how this performance came through me." Unknowingly though, they allowed Silence to unfold in their life, making such an expression of art possible.

During meditation, when we are simply present in our beingness, doing nothing, this state of receptivity allows Silence to unfold and express in our life.

What do we need to do for that?

Nothing!

So, do we "do" nothing?

No! We neither "do" nor "not do." We only remain present.

What do we "do" to drift to sleep at night?

Nothing at all! We are just present in a state that allows sleep to take over.

A little while before we go to sleep, we leave the living room and enter the bedroom. Then we leave the bedroom and find ourselves at bed. Soon, we leave the bed behind and wander about in our body and thoughts for a while. And then, slowly as thoughts subside, our focus eventually withdraws from our body and mind, and sleep takes over..

....

As soon as we become receptive to sleep and allow it to set in, sleep takes over, and we fall asleep. Similarly, we need to be receptive to Silence and allow it to take over.

Ironically, we do enter Silence every night when we are asleep. However, this does not bring about any transformation in our understanding because it happens in ignorance, without our awareness. The body undoubtedly gets recharged and feels fresh after sleep because of being in Silence.

When we experience Silence in the waking state, it transforms our life because we enter Silence with awareness. The goal is to allow Silence to unfold in our lives while we are awake. Daily practice of meditation makes this possible.

Just as the law of gravity states that water always gravitates downward, the **Principle of Silence states that Silence reveals itself when the dimensions of the body, *prana*, and thoughts are transcended.** When one goes beyond all these dimensions, one becomes a vehicle for the expression of Silence.

How can one go beyond the three dimensions?

The mind is the connecting thread between all these dimensions. Hence, we can go beyond these dimensions only when we detach from the mind. We need to prepare ourselves to rest in beingness and do nothing for this to happen. However, the mind poses hurdles in achieving this. The mind needs to completely give up all its attempts at "doing" and "not doing" to abide in Silence and allow its expression. It has to surrender unto Silence.

There is a simple and beautiful way of going beyond the mind and letting Silence unfold in life. It is the way of losing, of surrendering and allowing Silence to take over. Life then plays out on autopilot like a divine song.

It is essential to understand the meaning of surrender in the context of the awakening of Silence. Surrender of the mind is the bedrock for bringing harmony and spontaneity in life.

People carry many misconceptions about surrender, which make it difficult to understand its essence and relevance. When one hears the word "surrender," it raises a red flag in their minds. The logical mind feels as if one has to submit to someone or something. It perceives it as a form of weakness. People associate a negative notion with it. Deep within our belief system, surrender is fixated as a sign of defeat or giving up.

It is important to understand that we are not surrendering to a particular person, entity, or ideology, but to the Source of life itself. It is the way of awakening Silence to work wonders in life.

Life wins when we lose ourselves in Silence. When we learn to lose, we free ourselves from both victory and defeat—this is the paradox. Then nothing can defeat us in life, for we have already lost.

But the logical mind doesn't readily agree with this. It tries to reason, "How can one gain by losing?" The one who says, "I should control everything. Let me run the show," has to lose. By losing oneself, one needs to give in to the divine flow.

The auspicious wish to surrender is expressed in the prayer: "O God, let your divine will drive this life." As the seeker of Truth gradually understands this, he feels this is the most logical and straightforward thing to do.

Surrender makes it possible for Silence to unfold in life. With surrender, the mind serves like a flute—free from all its beliefs and inclinations—through which Silence plays its divine tune.

Questions for Contemplation

- Are you prepared to go beyond the dimensions of the body, *prana*, and thoughts?
- Are you willing to let go and train the mind to be prepared to lose?
- Do you prefer to lose in victory or to win by losing?

3

Tasting the Wordless Essence of Silence

Very few people strike the deal of surrendering the mind for the sake of Silence. However, this is indeed the best bargain that can ever happen in life. Here, Silence doesn't mean just keeping quiet. It refers to the conscious awareness that transcends both presence and absence of noise.

Before embarking on the journey of attaining this transcendental silence, let us understand its depth from the story of Mahakashyapa.

> Mahakashyapa was a disciple of the Buddha. Before meeting the Buddha, he was known as Kashyapa. This story is about the transformation of Kashyapa into the great Mahakashyapa.

During his first encounter with the Buddha, he urged him, "O Great Enlightened One! Please grace me with your wisdom."

The Buddha replied, "First, tell me what you don't know. Then I shall impart wisdom."

Kashyapa countered, "How does that matter? You have wisdom; please impart it to me."

The Buddha smiled, "It does matter. Until your state of readiness, intent, and purpose of seeking wisdom is not clear, imparting wisdom will be futile."

Kashyapa found it reasonable. He agreed and asked the Buddha, "How can I find what I don't know?"

The Buddha explained, "Write down all that you know on one side and all that you don't know on the other. There might also be something that you aren't sure of. Make a separate list of that too. In this way, divide all your knowledge into these three sections and bring them to me."

Kashyapa went back with a firm resolve and earnestly worked on dividing what he did or didn't know into the three sections as instructed. After he presented his findings, the Buddha bestowed wisdom on what he didn't know in due course of time.

After receiving this invaluable wisdom, Kashyapa gained clarity. He said, "I was in an illusion about what I believed I knew. I now realize that I know nothing at all. Besides learning what I didn't know, I find that all those answers that I believed I knew, all that I considered rationally true, have also proved wrong." ....
....

After attaining wisdom, Kashyapa received knowledge of his ignorance. The truth—**I know that I don't know**—dawned upon him.

Knowledge of one's ignorance is the precursor to wisdom. This is the first knowledge he received from the Buddha—the knowledge of what he *didn't* know. Only then could he become receptive to the wordless wisdom that the Buddha would transmit to him. Then it happened—the grand attainment for which all this preparation was on.

Once, all the monks were sitting in silence, waiting for the Buddha's arrival. He came, holding a lotus flower, and sat down. He kept gazing at the flower in silence without uttering a word. The monks were perplexed as this had never happened before. Till then, the Buddha's sermons had been discourses.

Kashyapa was also present for this sermon and observed what was happening. Suddenly a smile appeared on his face, and he prostrated at the very place where he was seated.

The Buddha then gestured Kashyapa to come forward. He handed the lotus to Kashyapa and then spoke to the others, "I have imparted to you, whatever can be said in words. That, which is beyond words, I have given to *Maha*kashyapa." Saying so, he ended the sermon.

There were old disciples and also some new ones present for the sermon. After the Buddha left, they started discussing what had just happened.

There was a disciple who took delight in intellectual prowess. He had noticed everything that happened but could not make any sense of it.

He approached Kashyapa and inquired, "What wisdom did you gain today?"

"It's so profound and subtle that words fall short of expressing it," exclaimed Kashyapa.

The disciple was not convinced. He continued his inquiry with some of the senior monks. They replied, "Profound wisdom has been given to us, but we are still contemplating it. We have understood some truths, but we need more time to understand it all."

The senior monks knew for sure that there was a secret in the Buddha's gesture of giving the lotus to Kashyapa. They needed to contemplate on it.

When the disciple approached some new disciples of the Sangha and posed the same question, they admitted their ignorance.

The disciple then considered directly approaching the Buddha. He waited for the right opportunity to meet the Buddha for gaining clarity.

Finally, when he got a chance to be alone with the Buddha, he asked, "O Master, people say that you have bestowed supreme wisdom and transformed Kashyapa to the stature of Mahakashyapa. I was present when you gave the lotus to Kashyapa. But I couldn't notice any such tangible transformation. If you have indeed imparted wisdom to him, please grace us too."

The Buddha replied, "First, delve deeper into your spiritual practice for some days. Practice meditation and render service in the Sangha. We shall talk about this later."

As instructed, the disciple continued his spiritual practice. He meditated, attended to the Sangha's activities, and rendered service. But whenever he was free, he would ponder, "What is that wisdom that the Buddha imparted to Mahakashyapa?"

When he could not hold back his curiosity any longer, he approached the Buddha yet again, "O Great One! I have dedicated myself to spiritual practice. I have a sharp intellect. I can now understand subtle concepts. I have understood the five principles of the *Panchsheel*. I have also grasped the sutra—*Buddham saranam gachhami*. I have understood the importance of surrendering to the Buddha. I have understood the purpose of seeking refuge in true dharma. I have grasped the import of the ten precepts.

"Now, please bless me with the wisdom that you imparted to Mahakashyapa in silence. Even if I am not able to grasp it, please give it a try."

The Buddha picked up a few fresh leaves from the ground and asked, "What is the color of these leaves?"

"They are green," replied the disciple instantly.

"How can you be so sure that they are green?" asked the Buddha.

"Anyone can say that they are green. When I was a child, my parents and teachers taught me that leaves are green," replied the disciple, without hesitation.

The Buddha smiled, "Had you been told since your childhood that the color of leaves is *blue*, then what would be the color of these leaves?"………………………………..

………………………………………………………………………………

The bolt of insight was instant and incisive. The disciple was dumbfounded. He finally said, "I am confused. Everything that I thought I knew is now questionable. I doubt whatever I have known. All I can say is that the leaf is in my realm of experience and it has a color, which I can see. I have grown to believe and hold onto whatever I was taught about that color since childhood. This much I am sure of."

The Buddha said, "Now you realize that the color you believed is not the real color. So then, what is the *actual* color of this leaf?"

"No, I cannot say that. If you remove the word 'green' from the color of the leaf, then what can I say?" replied the disciple.

Pointing at this profound insight, the Buddha spoke further, "You just called it a 'leaf.' Who has told you that it is a leaf? Had people around you called it a 'branch,' wouldn't it be a branch for you today?"

....

....

The disciple fell silent.

The Buddha continued, "Words are merely pointers. At best, they can point at reality; but they are not the reality. It is time to break free out of this matrix of words that you have lived in. Mahakashyapa was able to grasp this immediately as he was at the pinnacle of his spiritual practice. You also need to get into the very depth of your spiritual practice, mature in it, and reach its pinnacle. You need to uplift yourself through meditation and spiritual practice."

> The disciple fell at the Buddha's feet and begged for forgiveness. He said, "I am getting a faint sense of what you are hinting at. The intellect cannot grasp this profound wisdom. Instead of getting stuck in intellectual arguments and boasting about what I know, I will get into the depth of the truth beyond words."

The wordless wisdom that the Buddha imparted is like the sweet tasted by the dumb. ....
....

Just as a dumb person can taste sweetness but cannot describe it to anyone, one who has experienced Silence can alone understand it.

The knowledge of Silence cannot be transmitted in words. It can only be understood through direct experience. However, we can be pushed towards it with the help of stories, anecdotes, analogies, and pointers.

We will now begin our journey step-by-step towards Silence.

- In the first step, we will overcome our old ways of thinking so that they do not become obstacles in our journey.
- In the second step, we will overcome our emotions and tendencies so that they do not lower our receptivity.
- In the third step, we will build a strong foundation for Silence by deeply understanding who we truly are and the nuances of our mind.
- **At the fourth and final step, we will dwell in a state of surrender and let Silence experience itself and express its qualities.**

Now, let us embark on the first step towards Silence in the second part of this book.

Questions for Contemplation

- Do you know of your ignorance? Are you aware of what you really don't know?
- What are the beliefs you live by, which you need to get rid of?

PART 2
OBSTACLES IN REACHING SILENCE

Thoughts are like flares that arise in the sky of Silence. They appear for some time and then fade away. Witnessing the flares of thoughts can give us immense joy, but they don't because we don't see them as flares.

During festivals, we see fireworks lighting up the night sky. But if we think, "I cannot enjoy unless I light the flare myself," we cannot rejoice at the flares lit by others. Due to this constricted thinking, even a sky full of flares doesn't give us joy.

On the other hand, if we know the secret of happiness, we can become happy in every incident. Whether the flare of thought has arisen through our body or the other's, we will watch it with amazement.

If someone tells us, "I am getting such a thought," we exclaim, "Wow! Is that so? It is good that you are having such thoughts."

Nowadays, if you are getting thoughts like, "How do thoughts occur?" it is auspicious. Thoughts indicate the state of Silence within us.

4

The Two Possibilities of Thoughts

With every passing moment, in every incident, we have two options to respond:

- Respond from the state of Silence.
- Flow with the ongoing thought stream; the response emerges from the continuing current of thoughts.

Most of us usually choose the second option because we are unaware of the first option. We have learned to function through our minds since childhood, but we have not learned to recognize the Silence underlying everything. Hence, we are unaware of this ever-present Silence. We can choose the first option of responding from Silence only after we have recognized Silence.

Although words are inadequate to describe Silence, they can surely be used as pointers to hint at it. Thoughts serve as the bridge that leads to Silence.

Most thoughts pull us outward into the illusory world of the mind. They are thoughts like, "Let's go for shopping," "Whatever has happened with me is the worst thing," "No one cares for me," "It's not my mistake," "That person is to be blamed," and so on. Such thoughts trap us in the web of illusion.

However, certain thoughts pull us inward into Silence. They are thoughts like, "Who created this world?" "Where does the creator live?" "Does God exist in both bad and good people?" "I felt blissful after praying today," "I felt light and happy when I forgave my colleague," "I did not get what I prayed for, but it seems whatever happened was meant for my good," "Looks like the whole universe is working in my favor," and so on.

The kind of thoughts that occur to us determine where we are heading in life. ....
....

If we wish to progress towards Silence, we need to direct our thoughts consciously. This is possible only when we become free from the influence of illusory thoughts, our past conditioning, emotions, and personalized desires.

This part of the book helps us in breaking out of the web of illusory thoughts. As we break out of our thinking pattern, we will become more receptive to Silence. This receptivity will help Silence manifest in our life.

Questions for Contemplation

- Are you prepared to change the direction of your thoughts?
- Are you able to witness your thoughts by keeping a distance from them?

5

Frozen Thoughts

Just as water needs to flow, thoughts need to flow too. Flowing thoughts are always fresh. They allow life to flow spontaneously and beautifully. On the contrary, when thoughts freeze and stop flowing, they stagnate and pollute our thinking. Such rigid thinking gets etched in our mind and draws us away from the experience of Silence.

Frozen thoughts are stubborn thoughts that are adamant and resistant to change. Let us understand how these frozen thoughts affect our lives and how we can get rid of them.

> When people go on vacation, they leave an autoreply on their answering machine that helps callers know that they are away. Whoever calls for whatever reason, the answering machine gives the same pre-recorded reply

from memory. It cannot discern whether the caller wants to convey something urgent or important.

The answering machine in the above analogy symbolizes our body-mind, and the pre-recorded autoreply represents our frozen thoughts. We give fixed responses in every situation based on our pre-recorded thoughts. Most people use their frozen thoughts to respond in daily situations. It is time to do away with these frozen thoughts and respond afresh.

The formation of frozen thoughts

Innumerable thoughts arise in our mind from morning till night. Thoughts that spring forth spontaneously through intuition don't trouble us. But thoughts containing words like, "I, me, mine, we, you, yours, he, she, it, or they," come from the ego. Due to their continuous repetition, these thoughts get ingrained in our mind, becoming an integral and immovable part of it. They make our thinking stubborn.

Since childhood, we have been repeatedly told that we are this body. Hence, we have assumed it as the undisputable truth. We have repeatedly used "I" to refer to the body millions of times. With such repetition, the "I" that gets formed in a woman's body believes that it is feminine. The "I" thought that occurs in a man's body assumes that it is male.

The "I" also changes as per the relations with different people, professions, religions, countries, etc. It becomes a father, mother, brother, sister, aunt, grandfather, friend, colleague, employee, boss, Hindu, Muslim, Indian, American, etc.

Through the constant repetition of "I" as these identities, these assumptions and beliefs get frozen in the mind. These frozen thoughts give rise to a made-up personality. This personality is the ego, the false "I."

As infants, we neither had any ego nor the right understanding. We would treat both friends and foes alike. We would welcome and allow everyone. But as we grew up, we were gradually conditioned by ideas and beliefs that we received from our parents, teachers, neighbors, friends, and relatives. It resulted in the formation of frozen thoughts.

Frozen thoughts can also assume complex forms that form the basis for our limiting beliefs. They could be thoughts such as: "I don't have enough," "I don't deserve," "I always land up in a mess," "People cannot be trusted," "My work always gets delayed," "My happiness depends on what people feel about me," "I should always be right," etc. Such frozen thoughts become our core beliefs that infiltrate our perception and influence our responses.

Just as one safeguards and pampers their favorite child, we also safeguard our frozen thoughts and pamper our stubborn thinking by catering to their whims. We consider them as a reliable reference and try to tally every person or situation by using such frozen beliefs. When we receive recognition due to our frozen thoughts, we trust them even more; they get all the more reinforced. When things don't tally with them, we become unhappy. We try to blame or correct the concerned people or situations. Thus, we become happy or unhappy based on our frozen thoughts.

The fundamental purpose of the human body-mind

Given a flute, what would you do with it? You would surely try and play as many tunes as possible. Similarly, the human body-mind is a thinking mechanism for the Self. The Self uses this wondrous mechanism to think and express itself.

Think of the physically challenged people who cannot hear or speak. What will happen if an instrument were made available that would enable them to hear and speak? They would love to explore and use this instrument to the fullest to realize their full potential.

In the same way, the Self wants to experience itself and express its qualities using the body-mind. This is the whole and sole purpose of the human body-mind. We need to become receptive to Silence and allow the Self to express its fullest potential. ....
....

The Self can return onto itself through the practice of Self-inquiry by asking questions, such as, "Who am I? What am I? Why am I? Why am I associated with this body? Had this body-mind not existed, what would my state be?"

However, we have forgotten this fundamental purpose and considered ourselves to be the body-mind. As a result, we entertain thoughts, such as, "Why did this happen to me? He did this to me. They did that. How will my children settle in their career?" Constant repetition of thoughts containing "I, me, my, mine" has made our thinking stubborn. Such frozen thoughts have limited the expression of life.

If we want to freeze ice-cream, we first decide its flavor and then prepare to freeze it. But do we follow the same approach with our thoughts? No. Many of us often entertain precisely those thoughts that we do not want. These are thoughts of anger, hatred, envy, and anguish. Before entertaining such thoughts, we do not bother to ask ourselves, "What kind of thoughts do I like? Do I need such thoughts, or do I need some different thoughts to raise my consciousness?" If we truly love ourselves, we will question ourselves in this manner.

From morning till night, numerous thoughts arise in our mind, but not all thoughts trouble us. Many of them merely appear and subside. But the trouble is caused by those stubborn thoughts that do not align with the Self's purpose. The very fact that we feel troubled means that our thinking is based on our frozen thoughts. These thoughts distance us from the experience of Silence.

To attain the blissful state of Silence in all situations, we need to erase the past recording of frozen thoughts from the mind and record what we really want in life afresh. This new recording needs to be done with awareness and the right understanding so that it aligns with the Self's purpose. This will help us lead life happily and smoothly. Then the experience and expression of the Self will happen through our body-mind, and the real purpose of our body-mind will be fulfilled.

The first understanding that can help us in breaking free from frozen thoughts is: **We are not the body; we are distinct from it. The frozen thoughts pertain to the body. We have nothing to do with them.** The journey of Silence is about developing a conviction in this understanding.

If we do not consume ice-cream, it melts. In much the same way, if we investigate our frozen thoughts without *being consumed* by them, they dissolve. We need to inquire into each one of these frozen thoughts. Sorrow or unhappiness is an indication that the effect of frozen thoughts is consuming us. Hence, we should treat the feeling of unhappiness or sorrow as a feedback mechanism to doubt the very basis of our thoughts.

Like the police investigates a thief, we should consciously inquire into these thoughts by asking ourselves, "Who am I and what are these frozen thoughts? Do I really need them? What good have these thoughts done in life?" Such conscious inquiry will throw light on the fallacy and futility of these frozen thoughts. It will dissolve them, thereby allowing Silence to awaken.

We will realize that personality is nothing but a bundle of frozen thoughts. Every person around us is merely an expression of their frozen thoughts. Like the answering machine, their responses are dictated by their frozen thoughts. It is not that they are bad; it is just that they are habituated to use their frozen thoughts. If everyone gets rid of their frozen thoughts, then all communication and dealings will be from the Self to the Self! The Self alone will experience and express through everyone.

Questions for Contemplation

- What are the stubborn thoughts that drive your life?
- On what topics do you repeatedly think in the old preconceived way?

6

Recorded Thinking of the Past

You would have seen children play. If you carefully observe, a child always tries something new. He carries out several experiments throughout the day. While he succeeds at some, he fails at others. But he continues to experiment and takes delight in it without bothering about the outcome.

When the same child grows up, thoughts like "I know it all" get rooted in his mind, due to which he stops experimenting. Some people fall victim to such thoughts during their teenage while some during their twenties.

Soon, all experiences in life appear repetitive to them. Hence, they stop being receptive to the newness of the present moment. They begin to feel bored, depressed or perhaps even irritated. Some indulge in imaginary stories, some plan vacations, some get into unhealthy habits like smoking or drinking alcohol to escape these uncomfortable feelings.

Introspect honestly, "Is my present indeed a repetition of the past?" ....
....

The truth is that our present is not at all like our past. But the mind recalls the past from memory and repeats what it had done in the past. Due to this, it cannot grasp the newness that the present moment offers.

Whatever we have done in the past was based on our understanding then. We are different today vis-à-vis what we were in the past. Our understanding would have changed. Hence, we need to regard the present moment afresh. It is as if we are experiencing the present moment for the first time. How will that experience be?

We will experience the summer, winter, or the rainy season as if we are experiencing it for the first time. We will meet every person and perceive every object as if it is the first time. A trivial thing like looking into the mirror, or brushing teeth, will also become a wonder for us.

We will honor and rejoice at every incoming and outgoing breath. We will feel elated about the wealth of breath that keeps us alive! **The movement of breath is proof of our aliveness. It connects us to the experience of Silence within.**

However, our mind perceives the breath by referring to memory. Instead of looking at it afresh as an ever-new wonder of life, the mind sees it through the lens of past experiences. The mind looks at every person and object through the lens of past experiences associated with them and expects the same outcome in the present. We need to train ourselves to stop our mind from doing this.

You may have seen a bundle of sticks tied together. The mind, too, is but a bundle of thoughts tied together. In every incident, at every place, the mind keeps interrupting, as if saying, "See, it is my duty to remind you what happened here last time." Whenever we meet a person, the mind reminds us about how our previous meeting with that person was. It plays the past recording, "This person had not treated me well. How could she have done this? I felt disturbed after hearing that," and so on.

Whenever we visit any place or meet any person, it reminds us of how we had felt on the previous occasion. As a result, our outlook towards that person or place gets shaded by the past. We fail to see them as they are today and thus repeat the same past behavior.

When the mind intervenes in this way, we stop seeing the present experience as it is. We drift away from Silence and get into discord. The mind's habit of repeatedly reminding us of our past experiences puts us through immense trouble.

We need to be more aware of the play of the mind. Whenever the mind reminds us of past experiences, we should immediately discard it so that the mind becomes open to fresh thoughts.

If we do this, all our experiences from morning till night will be transformed into something magical. We will find each experience novel and unique. When we empty ourselves of all unnecessary thoughts and dwell in beingness, it helps us remain in the present moment.

Misery due to egoistic thoughts

When we keep repeating past thoughts, they give rise to egoistic thoughts that revolve around "I," "me," and "mine." For example, "I am right," "Don't blame me," "This thing is mine," and so on. When incidents do not align with our egoistic thoughts (expectations or desires), the ego feels hurt and miserable. Then we first try to rectify the incident or the person so that they align with our thoughts. But it is essential to understand that we don't have to rectify anything outside. Instead, we need to correct our thoughts and channel them in the right direction. Once we do this, we will observe every incident happily and accept it wholeheartedly. This heightened level of acceptance makes us more receptive to the experience of Silence.

Do we solve our problems by being happy or unhappy? If we are addressing our problems with an unhappy mindset, it means that we are looking at the problem from the lens of the ego. We perceive the problem from the reference point of egoistic thoughts. This point of reference is baseless.

We need to perceive every incident from the absolute standpoint of the Self—the experience of beingness that exists beyond thoughts. True spirituality is about realizing this point of reference. If our reference point is wrong, everything else will fall apart. At the end of life, we will realize that we have lived our entire life and perceived every situation from the wrong standpoint. We will discover that whatever we believed to be right was wrong; that we never doubted our ego; we never suspected our egoistic thoughts because of our constricted thinking.

There is a blind spot on the retina inside our eyes where no image can be seen. The human mind is like such a blind spot where the ego cannot be perceived. The ego is present, but the mind itself cannot spot it. True contentment can be attained in life only when we start doubting the doubting mind.

It is vital to cast doubts on our own mind, inquire about all its actions regularly, and notice all its exploits in our daily life. This daily introspection throws light on the effects of egoistic thinking in our life. **Even if we feel an iota of misery, know for sure that our egoistic thinking is overpowering us.**

Whatever we perceive and judge by using our egoistic thinking will eventually prove to be wrong. Hence, we should become receptive and abide in the experience of Silence at the very outset. As we dwell in Silence, the chatter of egoistic thoughts withers away.

But we see that everyone around us is also overpowered by their egoistic thinking. Hence, we feel that it is normal to function through our egoistic thoughts. Everyone conforms with whatever their ego says. We should first awaken the Self to stand apart and identify this thinking that is continuously going on in our heads. Otherwise, we will continue with the belief that this thinking is right.

We should re-look our egoistic thoughts and repeatedly ask ourselves, "Is my thinking right, or do I need to re-look at it?

With consistent introspection, our egoistic thinking begins to dissolve. Then a time would come when this thinking has completely dissolved. Thoughts would start arising from the Self, and there would be no interruption from the ego. All actions would happen directly from the Self. We will be free from the past and start living in the eternal present.

Questions for Contemplation

- In which situations does your mind linger in the past?
- In what aspects does your mind compare the present with the past?
- Which habits drift your mind away from Silence into the noise of worldly thoughts?
- Which thoughts create misery?
- From what standpoint do you perceive the situations in your life?

7

Past Happiness and Past Sorrow

Imagine you have traveled to a land where everything changes into something altogether different the next morning. For example, if you keep carrots in the fridge tonight, they might turn into radish tomorrow. If you place a bookmark in a book, it could change into a cloth-clip. Pens kept in the cupboard change into pencils. Pizzas kept in the oven emerge as burgers!

You find it troublesome to adjust to this new place. But you notice that the natives of this land are happy. You wonder how they can be comfortable and satisfied when everything around them is changing unpredictably. You then inquire about the reason for their happiness.

They disclose the secret, "We have accepted that every day is going to be different and we need to live with it.

Instead of unnecessarily getting upset about it, we have chosen to accept, allow, and live happily with whatever happens."

Gracefully accept and allow whatever happens—this is the secret of happiness. If we are unable to accept, we cannot be happy. Thoughts arising from the state of non-acceptance pose a hindrance in being receptive to Silence.

This different land is nothing but our mental world. When we place thoughts in our mental world, we cannot be sure about what will emerge tomorrow. We may strongly feel, "Things should turn out exactly as I think. Everything should fall into place tomorrow so that I can be happy."

But our mental world does not work that way. The solution is simple. We need to convince ourselves that we will accept whatever emerges in our mental world. We will then remain happy, no matter what. ....
....

We visit some friend, relative, or a place, and feel nice. Then our mind forms an impression of that pleasurable experience and expects to feel nice when we visit the same people or place the next time. If we had an unpleasant experience in the past, we expect the same experience this time and try to escape the discomfort. But it need not happen that way. Our experience could be different the next time. In situations where we expect to be happy, we may feel unhappy, or vice versa.

We don't need to compare our present joy with that of the past and reject it. Instead, we need to wholeheartedly receive and accept the joy that we experience in whatever way it unfolds.

In the above example, if we find a pencil in the pen's place, we will use it for writing. If we find a burger instead of the pizza, we will enjoy it. If radish is what carrots turn out to be, we will eat them with wonder.

If we feel miserable today, then we need to accept it as a fresh experience for today. We don't need to compare and connect it with the misery we have experienced in the past.

> For example, if a lady expects guests at home, she feels agitated by thinking about the ordeal she was put to during their previous visit. She recollects, "Last time, their kids had created such mess. They put the TV on high volume. They had scattered things all around the place. God knows what they will do this time."

Instead of lingering in such thoughts, she can choose to accept the situation completely. If the mind is not accepting the situation, she can choose to accept this non-acceptance as well. She can allow the situation to play out. She can let the guests come and then face whatever happens. She needs to keep her mind open to whatever unfolds this time.

It is possible that the guests may behave very nicely this time. But her past impressions of sorrow could intervene and prevent her from noticing this pleasant change. As her mind becomes open to new possibilities, she will be able to marvel at this change.

Even if they don't behave well, she will accept the sorrow instead of magnifying it by bringing in past impressions. She will see whatever happens in the new moment afresh.

When we are able to free the joy and sorrow of the present from past impressions, we can experience the present afresh. We would neither resist the present sorrow nor get attached to the present joy. For this to happen, we need to keep an open outlook. Once we develop this habit, we will experience joy intuitively flowing on its own. The mind will give up its stubbornness and Silence will get a chance to experience and express itself.

To keep an open perspective towards life, we need to tell ourselves, **"Now, I no longer insist on having the exact outcome as I had expected based on my preconceived notions (past impressions). I am prepared to enjoy whatever unfolds today. I will happily allow whatever emerges anew to come forth."**

In this way, our mind will get trained and develop the essential quality to allow Silence to blossom. We need to gain such mastery so that whenever the mind interferes with its past impressions, we should cast it aside by saying, "Now, there is no work left for you."

Attaining freedom from the past is one of the most important aspects of true spirituality. If we learn to live this way, we have understood a significant part of spirituality that we couldn't have otherwise realized, despite reading a thousand books of wisdom!

Questions for Contemplation

- Which miseries of the past do still affect you?
- How would your present be if it were freed from the past?

8

The Notion of Doer-ship

Nature is self-created, self-propelled, and spontaneous. This is a profound statement. One can spend one's entire life to grasp its essence. Everything is part of an auto-system. We can envisage how the cosmic orchestra is playing spontaneously. Nature does not merely comprise of planets, stars, galaxies, plants, trees, and animals, but also humans. This means human life is also happening spontaneously.

Every action is merely happening without a doer. But the egoistic mind doesn't agree to it. It believes, "I did this. I am the doer." This notion of doer-ship binds us with action, causing karmic bondage. When we truly understand that we are not the doer, we will see all actions happening spontaneously on autopilot. We will see all incidents playing out in the vast ocean of Silence. We will witness how our body wakes up, how it gets into activity, how thoughts arise, and so on.

To develop a conviction on this truth, we need to look back at our life since childhood. Who was running our life till we were two to three years old? As an infant, when we lied in our stroller and turned to a side, did we think and decide to turn over to one side? No, we didn't. Actions happened spontaneously without our conscious thinking. We instinctively turned to a side automatically.

When we began playing with toys, did we ponder, "Which toy should I play with today? How should I play?" No, we didn't. Playing and exploration happened spontaneously because we just remained in the state of natural flow. Then as we grew up to two to three years, the contrast mind began developing within us.

The contrast mind is that aspect of the human mind which judges and compares every incident and takes credit for everything that happens through the body. When an idea arises within us, we say, "I thought about it." But if we look closely, did we think of it, or did the thought occur to us?

No one can willfully bring forth ideas or thoughts. They spontaneously arise and pass through our awareness. When one realizes this secret, one starts becoming free from the notion of doer-ship.

Even something as trivial as giving a penny to someone is not up to us because we are not the doer. When we happen to see a beggar and give him a penny, why do we do it? A possible answer would be, "I gave the penny to the beggar because he was old, blind, and poor." But let's dig deeper and ask ourselves: Do we give away pennies to all the old, blind, and helpless people?

You may probably say, "No." A strong thought occurred, and you naturally felt like giving the penny to the beggar. If that thought hadn't occurred, you would have done something different. The beggar would have pleaded and gone off, without the least impact on you.

So, from where does the first thought arise?

It is time to contemplate where do thoughts come from. ....
....

Till today, we have considered that we are the doer, and we bring forth thoughts at our own will. But we are beginning to understand that this is not true. We do not bring forth the first thought. The first thought arises spontaneously from Silence. As soon as the first thought arises, action follows on its own. Later on, the mind believes, "I did this" and claims credit for this action. It considers itself the doer and is ignorant of the truth.

> Consider the example of a computer. When you click the [Start] button on the screen, a dozen more menu options pop up. Imagine that the computer begins to believe, "I have brought all these options up on my screen." What would you tell the computer? You would say, "You are a fool. If I had not pressed the [Start] button, these options wouldn't have popped up."

In the same way, we all are given the first thought. Without the first thought, no further thoughts can arise. Our brain can surely formulate ten more thoughts based on the first thought. But it does not have any power to create the first thought on its own. That's how the brain is designed.

What happens when you wake up in the morning? Do you first think, "It is time to wake up now"? Or do you just wake up? Think about it for a few moments before you answer. Is waking or not waking, up to you? Is it your choice?

If waking up was a choice, then nobody would die. Imagine a scene where a dead man is being taken to the cremation ground, and he thinks, "Okay, let me wake up now." And then he wakes up!

Absurd as this may sound, this cannot happen because no one has the power to bring the first thought on their own. When a person is dead, it means thoughts have stopped arising through his body-mind.

If the thought to wake up is not given to us in the morning, we cannot wake up. There are so many people who exist in a state of coma; some of them never wake up.

Our ancestors were aware of this. Hence, they would pray to God as the first thing in the morning after waking up, "O God, thank you for showing me a new day. Thank you for giving me the thought to wake up."

Even today, people offer prayers, but that understanding is missing. If that understanding were there, no one would live a stressful life. They would witness all incidents happening in their lives with wonder. All thoughts arising from the ocean of Silence would seem wondrous.

Iron pieces search for the magnet. They move close to it. When they are far from the magnet, they believe that they are on a journey in search of the magnet. But as they get closer, they realize that they were not searching for the magnet; the magnet was seeking them! The magnet was pulling them towards it all the while.

Similarly, we are not seeking Silence. Silence is pulling us towards it. In this journey, we do not attain Silence; instead, Silence unfolds through us. This understanding should deepen within us so that we can take each step in this inner journey towards Silence, knowing that we are being guided.

When the mind is convinced that all actions are happening instinctively and spontaneously on their own, it begins to lose its sense of doer-ship and stops taking credit for actions. It realizes that something beyond is the source of all thoughts and actions. It becomes more receptive to inspiration from Silence.

Questions for Contemplation

- In what situations does the sense of doer-ship arise within you?
- From where does the first thought arise? How many "first" thoughts do you get in a day?
- How can "first" thoughts arise more often?
- How does the notion of doer-ship pull you away from Silence?

PART 3
THE TRAPS OF THE MIND

Thoughts merely serve as news of our beingness, our living presence. Thoughts convey not only their content but also the state of awareness in which they arise. They convey the degree of awakening of the awareness, which is knowing these thoughts.

Thoughts of hatred indicate a deteriorated level of awareness. Thoughts like, "What are the divine qualities that the Self intends to express through this body-mind? How can these qualities find an expression?" indicate a heightened level of awareness.

9

The Web of Emotions

When favorable incidents happen in life, we experience a surge of positive feelings like love, joy, and gratitude. However, when we face adverse incidents, we feel a whole range of negative emotions like misery, fear, anger, hatred, anxiety, guilt, and resentment.

It is but natural to experience various emotions. They arise and subside. However, if we resist them instead of letting them flow naturally, they can accumulate in certain parts of our body and cause diseases. The occurrence of emotions is not as much a problem as their accumulation. Emotions slowly pile up and then get triggered at vulnerable moments to cause havoc within us. Just like frozen thoughts, these accumulated emotions also pose a hurdle in the experience of Silence.

Most people fail to understand how their negative emotions harm their bodies. When emotions arise, they find it difficult to stop their onslaught.

> For example, at the sudden demise of a close relative, one first feels a shock, fear, and despair. These emotions are either vented out as tears or suppressed. When one blocks these emotions, they experience numbness.

When we do not effectively deal with such emotions, they can deeply impregnate the body and cause chronic diseases.

Don't pamper your emotions

At the outset, when an emotion arises, it can be pictured as being lean and weak. But if we pamper it, it grows within us and penetrates deeper.

> When we check into a hotel room after a long journey, we put all our luggage aside and spread ourselves on the bed.

Similarly, emotions are like paying guests. When they arise in the body, they are slim and shriveled. But soon, they spread and grow because we commit the mistake of pampering them by indulging in them. ....

....

The mind indulges in negative emotions by weaving stories around them, such as, "No one values me. No one loves me. No one cares for me," and so on. These stories are food for the emotions to survive and thrive. It is as if we are feeding these guests with the food of stories instead of collecting rent from them!

The more the mind weaves stories, the more the associated emotion gets strengthened and becomes denser. Gradually, we begin to experience the physical effects of the emotion, like heaviness in the chest, shedding of tears, cramps in the belly, etc. Different emotions affect different parts of the body.

We have to tackle such emotions because they can make life a veritable hell and lower our awareness. Lowered awareness hampers our thought process, and we begin to attract undesirable things in our life. Hence, it is imperative to tackle these emotions and get rid of them

Let us understand some techniques to tackle negative emotions so that they don't affect us.

Focus on breathing

Our breathing changes with every emotion. By watching our breathing, we come to know the extent to which the negative emotion has affected us. When we listen to any bad news by holding our breath, the emotion enters into our system. Hence, on the onslaught of any negative emotion, we should focus our attention on our breathing. We don't need to control or regulate our breathing; instead, only watch it as it is. As our breath begins to normalize naturally, the emotion diminishes gradually. We may not see the result on the first day, but if we practice breath-watching daily, we will get to see its benefits.

Walk over emotions

Whether we are meditating or engrossed in activities, whenever an emotion arises, imagine that we are walking over the emotion.

Imagine we have written the names of all the emotions—whether positive or negative—on colorful card sheets and scattered them on the floor. Both positive and negative emotions, such as joy, fear, anger, guilt, hatred, pleasure, jealousy, sadness, boredom, depression, exhilaration, etc., have been laid on the floor.

Now, proudly walk over them with the understanding that being in Silence, we are riding the vehicle of our body over these emotions. This implies that emotions do not touch us but only touch our vehicle. We are only a witnesser. With regular practice of this technique, emotions will begin to reduce day-by-day. They will lose their power to lower our receptivity to Silence.

Release the emotion in the universe

Whenever any emotion arises, observe it and mentally size it up on a scale of 1 to 10 (ranking a mild emotion towards 1 and an intense emotion towards 10). Visualize the size of the emotion in 3-D. Size up the vessel that will be needed to hold the emotion and mentally place the emotion in the imaginary vessel. Mentally notice the color, texture, and smell of the emotion in the vessel. Throw the vessel with the emotion in the universe, thereby dissolving it in the wide expanse of deep space. You may need to repeat this process three to four times, every time feeling a reduction in the intensity of the emotion.

Watch the emotion with understanding

When we watch our emotions with the right understanding, alertness, and equanimity, they slowly diminish and ultimately vanish.

Emotions will arise in the body, but we don't have to justify or pamper them. We need to hold ourselves back from indulging in them. It is not necessary to consider them as the permanent truth and become sad. Instead, take a pause for some time.

Without affixing any "good" or "bad" labels to emotions, we need to watch them with equanimity. Such detached witnessing is based on the understanding, **"This emotion has now arisen in my body. I am only a witness to it. This emotion** is temporary—just as it has arisen, it will subside in some time. Let me keep watching its play while it lasts." In other words, we need to witness the emotion with the understanding that it is not happening with us. We are merely the knower of the emotion.

Witnessing the emotion with equanimity and understanding has many far-reaching benefits besides diminishing the present occurrence of that emotion. It helps in getting rid of other similar residual emotions that have accumulated in the body. Such witnessing also develops our maturity, confidence, and level of awareness. We become adept and confident at dealing with emotions.

Gradually, we become so proficient in this practice that every emotion will then remind us of being in Silence. Thus, emotions will then be "paying guests" in a true sense. They will pay us the rent of raising our awareness and help us abide in Silence. With this maturity, we will remain unaffected by emotions in any situation.

Question for Contemplation

- How will you tackle your emotions using the techniques given in this chapter?

10

The Stories of the Mind

What if you had two enemies, both pointing weapons at you. You can see only the first one's weapon. The other's weapon is invisible. Which of them would you consider more dangerous? Obviously, the second one. You can see the first one's weapon and gauge its distance from you, its intensity, and decide how to safeguard yourself. But what about the weapon that you cannot see? What can you do about it?

The mind also possesses an invisible weapon that poses hurdles in being in Silence. This invisible weapon is the mind's imaginary stories.

The mind weaves stories around the emotions that get triggered due to attachment or aversion. It thrives by feeding on these emotions and does not give them up easily. These stories influence the mind's ability to make decisions.

For example, most people often complain, "I could not meditate because I was tired." The mind has created this story based on its attachment to the body. It considers the body as the point of reference to make such decisions. Everyone feels tired after returning from a day's work or after a long journey. At such a time, no one will counter you if you lie down without meditating.

We can counter this by giving the mind a new reference point. We can tell the mind, "I need to meditate because I am tired." Unless we convince the mind with such counter-logic, it will not appreciate the importance of being in Silence. It will keep weaving stories driven by attachment or aversion.

If the body is indeed suffering from fatigue, you can still ask yourself, "Can I meditate while lying down?" When you witness the sensations arising in the body, you may find that not all parts of the body are tired as the mind had declared.

The mind makes decisions based on its stories and reacts accordingly. Instead, it should be trained to see the truth behind every situation before responding to it.

You would have seen that even after you are tired, your mind doesn't sleep immediately. It wastes time creating stories, such as, "He didn't behave well in the office. She shouldn't have said that. Everything lands in my workstack. I never get enough rest. The boss doesn't care about my situation. How am I going to complete this task," and so on. Such thoughts arouse anger or hatred towards others. Instead, you can use this opportunity for meditation.

If you need to accomplish a task, and your mind complains, "How should I accomplish this? I don't understand it. I cannot do it." Immediately question yourself, "What has exactly happened within me on thinking about this task? Why did I feel that I cannot do it? How did such a reaction arise within me?"

Such reflection will raise your awareness, and you will be able to make the right decision.

Question the basis of stories

The stories that we weave become the decision-makers of our life. ....
....

Once we are aware of this truth, we will become more vigilant. We will be able to see the invisible weapon in our enemy's hand and assess the harm it can cause us. Hence, we will choose to make decisions based on the truth instead of the stories created by the mind.

Let us understand how destructive this weapon of the mind can be with the help of an analogy.

> In many movies, they show the villain standing beside the hero. He cunningly slides his hand in his pocket and threatens the hero, "Be careful, I am holding a gun inside my pocket, pointing towards you. Better follow my orders, or else I will shoot you." The hero is unable to see the gun, but just because the villain has threatened him, he trusts his words out of fear.

In the same way, our mind points the weapon of its stories at us. We follow whatever the mind dictates based on its stories without verifying their authenticity.

This villain, in the form of the mind, orders us, "Shout at this person. Disagree with that person. Complain about that person. Eat whatever I ask you to." We agree with the orders of the mind and act accordingly.

To identify this hidden weapon of the mind, we need to have a penetrating ability to observe and see through the mind's working. The consistent practice of meditation helps us develop such a sharp ability to introspect the mind. It increases our sharpness, awareness, and alertness. We can then identify this subtle weapon of the mind and see through the farce that the mind plays.

It turns out that the imaginary weapon that the villain was using to threaten the hero was a harmless piece of stick. Most often, the so-called weapon that the mind uses to bring us down on our knees is also like this piece of stick, nothing more! But we still give in to its threats out of fear of getting endangered if we don't follow its diktats. Once we witness this weapon of the mind for what it truly is, we can confront this baseless fear. We will realize that the mind was not as powerful as we believed it to be!

Become free and then decide

All the stories of the mind are like mere bubbles in the air. They are hollow, with no truth. On the contrary, our life is based on the firm foundation of the truth. Hence, we need to make decisions based on the truth only and not based on the mind's hallucinations.

As we practice being in Silence, we become more alert and aware of the choices we make. We come to know the basis of our decisions. Was it the incident itself, or our attachment or aversion to it that drove our decision? Or was our decision a mere reaction to the sensations that arose in the body in response to the incident?

When we understand the real basis for our decisions, we can easily decide by keeping aside the feelings of attachment and aversion. It can then be said that we have made the decision from the state of freedom, from the right reference point.

The mind makes new compelling excuses every day and convinces us to do things against our will. For example, some people become victims of overeating. The thought of having food itself creates a pleasant feeling within them. Then they are oblivious of how much they eat. Later, they make excuses, "A friend had called me for dinner. I couldn't deny his loving invitation," or "A friend forced me to eat," and so on. If we keep a check on our emotions in such circumstances, our decisions can change. We won't fall prey to such urges and can discern our need to eat.

Hereafter, we need to assess our actions, the real reasons behind them, and to what extent our decisions are driven by the need to feel pleasant or to avoid feeling unpleasant. Once we are detached from pleasant or unpleasant feelings, only then can we truly become free to make the right decisions in our life.

Questions for Contemplation
- Which of your mistakes have you initially felt justified, but later proved to be wrong?
- What drives your decisions—the truth, or the stories of the mind?
- Contemplate on the situations you get stuck in the illusion of the world due to pleasant or unpleasant feelings.

11

The Trap of Attachment

There are two choices in life—freedom or bondage. This choice influences our decisions and our decisions shape our life. The choice of bondage draws us into the illusory web of *Maya*, whereas the choice of freedom helps us revel in the bliss of Silence.

We can understand the illusory play of Maya only when we vigilantly watch the traps of our mind. The most potent trap of the mind is attachment. The illusory Maya exploits this trap of attachment and coaxes us to do things we may have never wanted to, had we been aware.

When something is small, we can easily take care of it. But once it grows bigger, it becomes difficult to manage. And so it is with attachment. When attachment grows, handling it becomes difficult. As this is invisible, it is unknown to us.

In order to bring the unseen attachment to light, we need to question ourselves, "What am I attached to?" We will be amazed at the list of things we are attached to. We should also reflect on the real intentions behind whatever we do and assess whether attachment has any role to play in it.

We will find that we are fond of several topics. We are obsessed with our desires, ideas, and vices. We are also attached to our belongings and people.

Decisions taken without being aware of our attachments tend to go wrong. We then resort to excuses to justify our decisions. The mind is an expert in conceiving make-believe stories to justify whatever it says. We develop even more faith in these stories and get entangled in the maze of Maya.

If we do not unearth how this maze is working in our life, we will remain in ignorance. Once we identify these attachments, we can make the right decisions in life without being influenced by them. The practice of being in Silence makes us aware of our attachments. We should practice being in Silence not only with closed eyes but also with open and alert eyes in the ouside world.

Let us understand how attachment drives us.

Being attached to excitement

We like excitement, as it makes us feel alive. But we don't feel excited all the time; there are times when we feel bored. When boredom becomes intolerable, we try to bring back the feeling of excitement. We keep thinking, "What shall I do next? Where should I go? Shall I go for shopping? Shall I go out on a picnic? Shall I party with my friends?" and so on.

While indulging in these activities, we feel excited. The feeling of excitement throws a surge of happiness in our body, making us feel livelier. But it lasts only for some time. Soon, boredom sets in, forcing us to seek new avenues to boost our excitement.

There is nothing wrong in going to parties or attending family functions as a part of our social responsibility. But if we are obsessed about it, it poses a hurdle to be in Silence.

Most people are unaware of their attachment to excitement. They fail to understand, "Why do I feel dull and bored when there is nothing to do? Why do I feel depressed? Why don't I feel happy?"

In this blind race of feeling high and excited, people do not see their mind standing right before them, wielding this weapon of attachment, due to which they feel depressed. They need to break this attachment to come out of this maze.

Usually, no one can compel us to do anything against our will. But this is not the case with our mind. The mind craves excitement and compels us to do things which we wouldn't otherwise. We continue to pursue various avenues to feel excited. Just think about it—how much we harm ourselves in the process of indulging in excitement. ………………………………
………………………………………………………………………………

Attachment to appreciation

We feel like having more of whatever we like. If someone praises us for something, we long for even more appreciation.

Without realizing it, most of us keep seeking appreciation from others, being in their good books, and being honored. If we look around, we find that Maya is mockingly playing her game and fooling everyone.

If we aspire to be free from this maze, we need to ask ourselves, "What do I achieve by being enslaved to appreciation from others? Is whatever I have gained permanent?" ……………………
………………………………………………………………………………

If whatever we gain from seeking appreciation is permanent, then it would be worth indulging in it. But the truth is the opposite. The pleasure derived from appreciation lasts only for a short time, as long as we continue to linger in it. Soon, we set out in search of yet another pursuit of pleasure.

Permanent happiness resides within us. But instead of seeking it within, we seek it in the outside world and are convinced that whatever we are doing is right. We get deluded by the illusion of Maya. If we break free of it, we can progress towards true freedom that can be found in Silence.

We have to make a choice—whether to plead people for appreciation, or dwell in Silence and be free from this maze of attachment to appreciation. If we choose to be free, we will remain happy forever, whether we are appreciated or not. If we receive appreciation, it will merely be a bonus, but we won't crave for it.

Questions to ponder

We need to question ourselves, "What is the real intention behind the great actions happening in the world? Are they done from the need for excitement or as part of leading a genuinely selfless life? Whatever I am doing, is it owing to freedom or bondage?"

If we honestly answer these questions, it will help throw light on our attachments. The virtue of honesty is essential for every sincere truth-seeker. This introspection will help us overcome our attachments. But this cannot happen forcefully. Our aspiration to be free from this enslavement and our growing love for freedom will make it happen automatically for us. We will stop attending to things that enslave us. Even if we need to associate with them, we will be vigilant not to get stuck in them for long.

Whenever we catch ourselves telling a lie, gossiping about someone, taking a wrong decision driven by attachment, or falling prey to excitements, we should understand that we are enslaved to excitement and our receptivity for Silence has reduced.

We can then increase our receptivity by working in favor of the truth and break free of this bondage. Our choice of freedom will soon help us revel in the bliss of Silence and experience true freedom.

Questions for Contemplation
- What are the various things that you are attached to?
- What has been the basis for your decisions until today?
- What will be the basis for your decisions hereafter?

12

Demonic Tendencies

Tendencies are inclinations that compel us to follow certain fixed patterns of behavior. They pull us towards the illusory world of Maya and deprive us from being in Silence.

Pareto's principle, also known as the 80/20 rule, applies to our tendencies too. 20% of our tendencies cause us 80% harm. Our job is to identify and work on each of these 20% tendencies.

....

What are these tendencies, and how do they function? Let us understand this with the help of an example.

> There were two friends who were also colleagues at their workplace. One of them knew the job of plumbing very well. He had done plumbing work many years ago. Let us call him "the plumber friend" and the other "the non-plumber friend" for an easy reference.

One day, they traveled together to another office for an important meeting. As they reached the office, they saw a beautiful garden. Then suddenly, both of them noticed a leaking water tap. The non-plumber friend immediately shifted his attention to the meeting venue. However, the plumber friend's eyes were glued to the tap due to his tendency.

He couldn't hold himself back and went on to fix the tap. He checked the tap thoroughly, found the source of the leakage, and then unscrewed the tap. He tied a thread around the tap windings to arrest the leak. Thus, he got busy with this task.

When he joined the meeting, only five minutes were left for the meeting to end. He was disappointed at having forgotten his real purpose of being there. His friend adviced him, "You had come here to attend the meeting. You should have focused on that alone."

The plumber friend replied, "What could I have done? Whenever I see a leaking tap, I just can't hold myself back."

This is not some plumber's story, but our own. This happens with many of us. Most of us tend to get stuck in things that trigger our tendencies, which draw us away from Silence. We need to reflect: In which scenes do I find it difficult to hold myself back? What are the tendencies that distract me and disrupt my practice of Silence?

Just like the plumber, we get involved in unnecessary scenes because of tendencies, and by the time we are back to our actual goal, we are left with no time or energy.

Our tendencies can break the consistency of our spiritual practice. The tendency that breaks our consistency can be considered demonic.

Since the ancient times, these demonic tendencies have been regarded as the gravest sin. In Indian mythology, demons were known to cause havoc and disrupt the austere practices of sages and saints. In the same way, these demonic tendencies disrupt our practice of Silence.

Tendencies can be very subtle and hideous in their design. They seem very convincing to us, due to which we fall for them when our awareness is low. We soon find ourselves in their maze, without realizing it.

We need to raise our awareness to annihilate such demonic tendencies. Whenever tendencies arise, we need to consciously shift our focus away from them and dwell in Silence. Tendencies that are ingrained within us since many years can be stubborn. They keep coming back and drawing our focus. Hence, the spiritual practice of shifting our focus away from them has to be rigorously and consistently practiced.

With right understanding, perseverance, and devotedness, the very tendencies that were pulling us away from Silence will begin to serve as reminders to return to Silence.

Questions for Contemplation

- Which of my tendencies pull me away from Silence? (e.g., laziness, anger, procrastination, etc.)
- Which of my tendencies harm others?

13

The Stages of True Detachment

There lived a Sufi saint in Baghdad, who was renowned far and wide for his wisdom. Many people used to come from faraway places to meet him and discuss spirituality.

One day, an ascetic came to meet him. Having heard a lot about the saint, he was eager to meet him and waited for his turn.

When his turn came, the ascetic was invited to the saint's meeting hall. He was awestruck by the arrangements there. The saint was living in a plush mansion. Many volunteers were serving him. Guests were warmly welcomed and served delicious food. Costly mattresses were laid on the floor where spiritual discussions would take place. Velvet curtains rolled over the windows and doors. Bells hanging from the ceiling would chime melodiously in the breeze.

The ascetic noticed all this and pondered, "Can someone who is used to living in such luxury be a saint? This place is not suitable for an ascetic like me. I'd better leave this place."

Just when he was about to leave, the saint arrived and stopped him. The saint asked, "If you have come to meet me, then why are you leaving?"

The ascetic replied, "I had come to learn something from you. But I noticed that you are attached to worldly pleasures. I am far better off. What will I learn from you? We can learn only from someone better than us. Hence, I am leaving."

The saint promptly replied, "If you are better than me, I must learn from you. Please accept me as your disciple. I am prepared to renounce everything immediately and come with you."

The ascetic was shocked to hear this. He allowed the saint to accompany him. The saint instantly bid farewell to his disciples and his grand mansion and accompanied the ascetic.

They had only walked a short distance when the ascetic suddenly remembered of his water-pot. He had forgotten it at the saint's meeting hall. He immediately requested the saint that they should return to fetch his water-pot.

The saint replied, "I didn't take a second to renounce that grand mansion and leave with you. I didn't feel any attachment to my devotees either, because I know for sure that whoever needs me will surely find me. And you want to go back for a little pot! I didn't have the slightest attachment for the grand mansion, and you are so attached to your water-pot?"

This was an eye-opener for the ascetic. He could witness his attachment and realized how much he needed to work on himself. He fell at the saint's feet and begged his forgiveness. He became the saint's disciple and attained wisdom.

We get attached to whatever actions we perform. We are not attached to the plants or trees we watch while walking on the street. But when we plant a seed in our garden, we get attached to it. Looking at the plant, we always think, "*I* have planted this." If someone harms it or claims to own it, we feel hurt. This binding is nothing but attachment.

When we become free from all attachments, our body-mind becomes receptive to Silence. Let us understand five stages in the journey towards true detachment.

Excessive attachment

This is an intense form of attachment. When we suffer from excessive attachment, we remain blind to our own mistakes, even when it is visible to everyone else.

In the Mahabharata, King Dhritarashtra was deeply attached to his sons due to which he not only ignored the injustice done to the Pandavas but also did nothing to stop the brutality meted out to Draupadi.

History is replete with examples of such excessive attachment. Knowing them, we should understand how attachment can draw us into the abyss of bondage and take precautionary measures well in advance.

Reduced attachment

The adverse incidents of life can help us reduce our attachment to people and situations. In some situations, we always depend on others. We believe, "I will be happy only if this happens. I can complete my task only if this person helps me." People can take advantage of our condition due to our lack of self-reliance.

When such incidents happen, we initially feel sad. We grumble why they happen with us alone. But we need to understand that these adverse incidents can help us get rid of our sorrow. They don't come to sadden us but to help us awaken and progress in life. The grand vision of nature is to elevate us to a higher level of consciousness with every incident.

> Many people died in the world war. Looking at the melancholy and torture in the war, people awakened to the need for world peace. This unfolded the next scene of a warless world.
>
> People misuse water. But when rainfall is scanty and water supply reduces, they become aware of the prudent use of water. Then they start rainwater harvesting, plan for water storage, etc.

Thus, incidents can awaken people and reduce their attachment. Some people learn by reflecting on the futility of holding onto their attachments. Those who become bitter, hateful, and egoistic when weathered by incidents don't learn their lessons. Their attachments keep increasing.

Shaken attachment

Some people experience relief when their attachments reduce. But then, they don't progress further in their journey of detachment. But exalted souls like the Buddha do not stop at this juncture.

> When Prince Siddhartha caught sight of a diseased person, an old person, and a corpse, these incidents shook his attachment towards the world and his own body. It brought about a complete transformation in his life. It compelled him to relinquish his palatial comforts and loved ones in search of the ultimate truth. At the pinnacle of his spiritual quest, he became the Enlightened One. Thereafter, he dedicated his life to the service of awakening mankind.

When the attachment to the body and its possessions breaks, one is inspired to make such powerful decisions. This stage can be called shaken attachment.

Just like the life of Prince Siddhartha, a mere indication is enough to propel some people towards being rooted in Silence. Some others gain understanding only after repeatedly going through incidents.

> At the age of sixteen years, when Sri Ramana Maharshi experienced the fear of impending death, he was instantly transported into the state of *Samadhi*. All attachment to the body was severed during that incident. He remained rooted in the Self without any expression for a long period.

Such examples inspire us to lead a life without attachment. A coconut's dried kernel detaches from its shell and can be easily taken out after breaking the shell. Similarly, while staying in the world amidst people and situations, we need to develop detachment towards them.

Detachment from attachment

At this stage, we develop detachment from attachment. Most of us are attached to our belongings. Due to this attachment, we don't dispose things that we don't need from our house. These unnecessary things keep piling up. We buy new things but do not discard old ones. We need to re-think from time-to-time and abandon some of them to get detached from them. We need to honestly reflect, "Am I using these things, or are they using me? Who owns whom?"

What happens with our belongings outside also happens with our thoughts inside. We have accumulated past thoughts within us due to attachment. Just as we clean our house, we also need to clear the pent-up emotions and memories that do not serve us. We need to seek forgiveness from others and also forgive them. Even if we feel like crying, we should. All the past clutter will flow out with it. Keeping ourselves clean from within is indeed an art. This helps us detach ourselves from old thoughts and become free. By freeing ourselves within, we become receptive to Silence.

Detachment from detachment by being in Silence

After developing detachment, we can become attached to detachment itself! Many people get stuck here. We need to break this attachment to detachment for progressing further.

> Many housewives find it hard to throw things away. They are attached to things. But as they start getting rid of them, they find their house meticulously clean. But now, they immediately get angry if someone misplaces things. They wish to have their house always clean and tidy with everything at its place at all times. They become attached to cleanliness and the tools used for cleaning. Cleanliness becomes an obsession for them.

Virtuous people get trapped in such situations. Initially, they may have been ignorant. But when they receive wisdom, they develop an ego of their wisdom.

Being virtuous is not the final stage in the journey of detachment. There is yet another stage of going beyond the states of lethargy, hyperactivity, and virtuousness. It is the state of detachment from detachment, which is devoid of all inclinations. We need to work towards transcending virtuousness as well.

Initially, the illusory Maya traps us in the form of vices that we can identify and get rid of. But later, Maya uses the words of wisdom and tries to sneak in through the backdoor. It is as if Maya is saying, "If you can spot whatever is black, then I will enter as whiteness." It is not easy to spot this subtle trap that Maya lays for us.

We need to raise our awareness to be able to see through this and detach from words of wisdom as well. Go beyond both black and white, and focus attention on the colorless screen on which both black and white appear. We can then playfully watch the game of opposites.

When we get rid of our attachment to detachment, we attain the state of absolute detachment, where we dwell in Silence.

Questions for Contemplation
- What are your attachments?
- What experiments can you perform to attain absolute detachment in Silence?

14

The Maze of Desires

I await that desire, which will free me from all desires.

One of the greatest misunderstandings that most people have is that they cannot accomplish any work without having a desire for it. This is far from the truth.

The problem with desires is that we feel sad and troubled when it appears that our desires are not being fulfilled. Our mind casts doubts such as, "I don't know whether this desire will be fulfilled or not?" Such doubts make our wait for gratification of desires seemingly endless. Sadness resulting from unfulfilled desires is an obstacle in being receptive to Silence.

Desires shape our life, and then life shapes our desires. Ultimately, desires drive our life.

We consider ourselves an individual body and harbor only personalized desires instead of wishing well for humanity at large. Gradually, such desires become predominant and start driving our lives. Thus, we lead a constrained life, enslaved by our desires.

A wife once told her husband, "If I die before you, don't mention my age in my obituary."

What kind of desire is this? People entertain such futile desires that become the whole and sole goal of their life. They do not think beyond it.

If we introspect deeply, we will encounter such futile desires within us too. We have not received this life to fulfill such petty desires. We are here to complete the ultimate wish of realizing our real Self, to attain Self-realization.

It is time to get rid of all futile desires that we have entertained in our free time and got habituated to. These desires pull us away from the bliss of Silence. ....

....

Not even a single desire that can pull us away from Silence should remain. Now, let us understand the secret of fulfilling desires without desiring them.

Whether we desire or not, Nature continuously supports and provides for our progress. Even if we don't desire, Nature drives us to accomplish relevant actions that propel us towards our growth.

We can achieve whatever we desire, even without entertaining those desires! When we do not have any doubts about a desire, the desire does not bother us. This doubtless state can be easily attained in Silence. We become receptive to the experience of the Self in this state.

When we are present in a relaxed state without any desires, we become a magnet. In this state, all desires, according to our divine plan, are fulfilled on their own automatically.

But how can we be present like a magnet? Sometimes it so happens that we are working on a task, and we are not sure about its completion. We cannot say for sure when it will be completed. We get stressed about it.

At such times of uncertainty, we can tell ourselves, "Let me see what happens next." After that, we dwell in the state of waiting in Silence. We need to be in this state, unconditionally waiting for the next scene to unfold. We don't have any fixations about the outcome. It is a paradox how this desireless state catalyzes the fulfillment of whatever is best for us as per our divine plan.

In this waiting state, we don't insist on completing the work faster or better. While we engage in action, we mentally wait by saying, "Let me see what happens." We perform all the requisite tasks, but remain in a waiting state that arises when we are free from all desires. We wait for everything in general and nothing in particular. Just imagine how our life would be if we were free from the pull of all desires!

Questions for Contemplation

- Based on the understanding from this chapter, when a desire arises, how will you regard it?
- How prepared are you to be present in a state free from all desires?

PART 4
AWAKENING OF THE REAL I

It is auspicious to be in a thoughtless state, even for a few moments. We don't have to obtain this state from elsewhere. With understanding, we realize that the thoughtless state exists from the very beginning. Thoughts arise from this state and subside in it. Abiding in this state does not mean that there won't be any thoughts. Thoughts will arise and drive the body into action. But we will be ever aware that we exist in the thoughtless state, whether the body is still or in activity.

15

The Real Character in the Present

You may have seen photo studios at fairs. They have a variety of costumes such as that of a lawyer, an inspector, a doctor, a farmer, a soldier, etc. People are fond of taking their pictures in these costumes. When they wear them and pose in front of the camera, the photographer says, "Smile, please."

Life is also like a fair, wherein we keep wearing various costumes! Now, what are these costumes? And who is the photographer?

The sense of beingness is ever-present. It is life itself! It is constantly aware of everything that is being known. It is the photographer who keeps observing various costumes that we adorn. Whenever we feel unhappy, life smiles back at us and says, "Right now, you have worn the costume of an unhappy person. Your picture has been taken. But the 'real' you is not unhappy. Now, come out of this unhappy person's character and smile, please!"

So, life asks us to smile *after* the picture has been taken!

The body and mind are our costumes. Who-we-truly-are has worn these costumes.

There are countless bodies on Earth. The Self, which is common in all these bodies, wishes to express itself through these innumerably different bodies.

Consider that the Self wants to take its own pictures in the vast variety of costumes—sometimes in the unkempt costume of a bored person, sometimes in the red costume of an angry person, at times in the green costume of an envious person, the black costume of someone who is depressed, the grey costume of a confused person, the blue costume of joy, the pink costume of excitement, and so forth.

The Self is constantly watching from within. It tells, "The picture is taken. Now come out of the character, and smile, please!"

The smile that emerges when we step out of the conditioning of the body and mind indicates that we are becoming receptive to Silence. Our picture in a bored person's costume has been taken. Now come out of boredom, and smile, please!

We play various roles throughout the day. They could be the role of an angry person, someone filled with hatred, someone who is jealous, someone who is playful, or someone who is helpful, and so forth. As soon as we complete the role, we should return to our original state of being in Silence.

We don't have to get stuck in any role any longer than required. Neither do we need to remain stuck with our emotions, particularly negative emotions such as anger, hatred, envy, etc. At least after we have worn these costumes, we need to ensure that we come out of them and dwell in Silence.

But everything begins to go wrong when the Self assumes, "I am this body... I am this mind." It then identifies itself with the body and the mind and gets stuck in the character's story. The Self believes that whatever happens to the body or mind is happening to itself. ....
....

We need to learn our lessons in every problem, in every situation. Once the problem is resolved, we need to get back to our original nature of Silence. When we are out of the character-costumes, we are the pure, formless, boundless presence. Now, the smile that radiates from this presence will be our original smile.

Whether the costume is of a negative or positive feeling, we are out of it. We *are* the Silence in which costumes are worn. Let us understand how to practice this in everyday life with the help of a story.

Who am I now?

> Amar was desperately searching for a job but had no success despite his best efforts. He was struggling. Then he suddenly remembered his friend Ravi, who was working abroad. He called Ravi, explained his situation, and requested him to search a job for him.
>
> Ravi assured him, "You can come down here. I will surely find a good job for you."
>
> Overjoyed and also a bit anxious, Amar asked, "I don't have any prior experience of working overseas. Can I get some special training for the job?"

Ravi clarified, "Sure. Why not? You just come here at the earliest. I will take care of everything else."

Amar replied, "Ok, I will try my best to reach there as early as I can. But tell me where, when, and how should I come after I land there?"

Ravi informed, "Come to this particular hotel at 10 p.m. next Monday. I will meet you at a gala function organized there."

Amar asked him, "What should I do if I don't meet you there? I don't understand the native language. I might find a big problem conversing with people there."

Ravi immediately clarified, "Don't worry. If you have any problem or anyone enquires anything, just say, 'WAIN' and your problem will be solved."

The following Monday, Amar landed in Ravi's country. But due to the time difference, he reached at 10 a.m. instead of 10 p.m. Now, he started looking for Ravi, but couldn't find him.

Then he realized his mistake about the time zone difference. He was in a dilemma as to how he would spend the whole day. Just then, a native person approached him and complained about something in the local language. Amar couldn't follow anything.

He immediately recalled what Ravi had told him and said, "WAIN." The native person quickly nodded and went away. Amar was relieved.

Now he started wandering around, checking out the city streets. When he entered a café, a waiter walked up to him and told him something in the native language. Again, Amar was confused. He again repeated the mantra, "WAIN." To his surprise, the waiter went away at once.

When Ravi reached the hotel at night, he was amazed to find Amar playing happily with some kids. Then Amar explained what had happened since morning. By the time the function was over, it was midnight. Ravi arranged for a room for Amar in the same hotel.

The next morning, Ravi found that Amar was busy helping the hotel staff in the reception. He was also speaking to the guests of the hotel. Ravi was overjoyed seeing this.

He approached Amar, "Looks like you have already got accustomed to the people and settled down here. You are mingling with everyone so easily."

Amar happily replied, "Yes, I am enjoying this place. Now tell me about my job and what kind of training I am required to undergo."

Ravi laughed heartily, "You are already on the job and have got trained as well. I thought of you for the position of a manager in this hotel. I see that you are already doing that job very well as per expectations."

Amar was overjoyed. He thanked Ravi from the bottom of his heart.

This analogy might have raised some questions in your mind. Amar was so anxious in the beginning. What kind of training did he undertake in just one day, which made him so comfortable in the foreign land?

The answer is **"WAIN – Who am I now?"** This question will help you come out of your costume. It will awaken you and bring you in the present moment.

The problems that Amar faced in the story represent common occurrences in our daily lives. Let's understand this.

Many times, we fail to understand what the other person wants to convey. We misinterpret and misunderstand it. For example, when the other person looks at us in a particular way, we may feel that he is angry. If he doesn't respond as we expect, we assume that he is behaving rudely. If he disagrees with us, we may conclude that he disrespects us. If our friend doesn't help us in a given situation, we may consider that he is not our true friend. If our close ones do not listen to us, we might feel that we are not being loved. If the boss rejects our idea, we might assume that the boss considers us worthless. Generally, people often face such situations in life.

Just like Amar, we also need to take the support of the mantra "WAIN." When we ask, "Who am I now?" it brings us in the present.

We have been progressing step by step towards Silence over the last few chapters. In this journey, we first worked upon our thoughts, then our emotions and tendencies. Now we have reached a stage where we can bring ourselves back in the present by asking, "Who am I now?"

The present is the only place where we can experience bliss. Perhaps, that's why it has been called the "present." We become receptive to Silence in the present. Silence gets an opportunity to reveal itself in the present. Thus, being in the present is the easiest way for Silence to be revealed. Let's understand when and how we can ask WAIN.

When emotions arise in any situation, ask yourself, "Who was I a moment back? What costume had I worn?" The answer could be, "A moment back, I was a reserved person; I was a troubled person; I was a bored person; I was confused; I was angry; I was egoistic; I indulged in comparison, and so on."

Now, ask yourself, "Who am I now?" As soon as you ask this question, you will find yourself in the present moment, out of the costume of the character who was feeling those emotions. **The moment you remember, "Who am I now?" you immediately return to the real I in Silence.** You will then see that the problem dissolves.

What was Amar doing from 10 a.m. till 10 p.m.? He was practicing meditation. He asked, "WAIN – Who am I now?" in all situations and abided in the sense of beingness.

When the person outside the airport or the waiter in the café came and asked him something, Amar chanted "WAIN," and they nodded and left. What does it mean for us in our everyday life? It does not mean that challenging situations will cease to occur or change according to the mind's fancies.

It means that **we will stop being attached to the character that is stuck in the situation.** A moment ago, Amar had worn the costume of confusion, but as soon as he asked himself "WAIN," he was back in the present, in Silence. He was detached, not just from the situation, but also from the character within him who was in the situation.

If you ask, "Who am I now?" in every situation, you will steer clear from various character costumes and their associated emotions and constantly remain in Silence. This way, you can make the right decisions from the freedom of being in Silence.

Questions for Contemplation

- In which costumes have you taken your pictures today?
- Ask yourself, "Who was I a moment ago? What was I doing a moment ago? What was I thinking a moment ago? And who am I now?"

16

Attacking the Root Belief

The belief that we are the costume that we wear keeps us identified with it. We spend our entire life believing that we are this body. We remain bereft of the experience of the Self. We cannot imagine that we have a formless existence—the real "I" without any form or face. Attachment to facial appearances is so deeply entrenched in the mind that considering an existence without a face, without a persona, seems impossible.

> An artist first creates an outline on canvas before filling it with colors and shades.

The human body is also just an outline drawn on the canvas of Silence; it is not the complete picture. When we are attached to this body, it limits our existence. What is limitless and boundless, gets bound and constrained.

Every night, when we drift to sleep, we lose the sense of the body. We do not remain limited by the outline of the body. We wander about in the dream world. When we wake up in the morning, we state, "I slept well!"

Everyone wishes to lose the sense of the body. It is only after we become free from the limitation of the body that we attain pure bliss. However, we identify with our body-mind and assume we are the body-mind. As soon as we break free from this attachment to the body and mind, we experience pure joy. This also happens during any activity that we are engrossed in.

> When we play our favorite sport, we can be so engrossed in it that we wouldn't notice if our leg suddenly hit a sharp object and started bleeding. We could be oblivious of the wound until someone spots it and informs us. But the moment we notice the wound, we immediately start feeling the pain. We wouldn't have felt the painful sensation earlier because our mind was absorbed in the game. When our mind notices the wound, it associates a thought, "I am the body" with the wound. The mind paints an illusion, "*I am wounded and bleeding.*" As a result, we begin to experience anguish due to the pain.

The mind dissolves when we fall asleep and comes back into existence when we wake up. Sleep happens only when the mind does not exist. But then, the mind announces, "I was present in the sleep." We get fooled by this belief of the mind.

Pure joy is experienced only when the mind is absent. But the mind doesn't agree with its non-existence. It always believes and proclaims, "I was there when joy was felt."

> Someone is giving a musical performance and the audience applauds when the performance is at its peak. The musician feels very happy and attributes her happiness to the applause. But that is not the truth.

When the performance is at its peak, only the performance is happening. Her mind is completely immersed in the performance. This is the real cause of her joy. She breaks free from the limitations of her body-mind and becomes limitless. This makes her happy.

But her mind comes back later and claims that it was present during the performance. It even claims the joy and credit for the performance!

Musicians love to be lost at the peak of their performance. The real joy that they experience is because the mind drops, and Silence is experienced. However, as this is not understood clearly, they believe that their performance or the audience's applause gives them joy.

When we lose our identification with the body-mind, we come out of the darkness of stupor and rest in the light of awareness.

The mind needs a weapon to infuse stupor. The "I" thought is its weapon. The occurrence of the "I" thought immediately separates us from the state of Silence. **As the "I" thought arises inside the body, the real "I" believes, "I am this body." However, the body is just an instrument. The moment the real "I" identifies itself as the body, a separate individual *seems to* exist.** The mind repeatedly plays this game and succeeds in creating an illusion.

Suppose you say "I" through a mike. You believe that the mike is saying "I" and get deluded. Hence, you assume, "I am this mike, which is speaking." Thus, you get identified with the mike as "I." In this example, you can clearly see who is speaking. The mike is just a medium through which you are speaking.

In the same way, the body is just a medium through which the real "I" speaks. But as the "I" thought arises through the body, the real "I" believes, "I am this body, and this body is speaking." As a result of this belief, the real "I" (which we truly are) immediately drifts away from its true nature of Silence and identifies with the body, the false "I." This "I" thought then gives rise to many more thoughts based on body-identification, thus giving birth to the mind, and this game continues.

Now, it's time to reverse this game. We need to shift from our body-identification and trace it back to the "I" thought that causes this identification. Further, we need to shift from this "I" thought to Silence (the real "I"). We need right understanding to return to Silence. Indeed, understanding alone can lead us to Silence. Understanding helps us dwell in the silent (thoughtless) awareness that exists beneath (beyond) all thoughts.

Every incident and every experience in life serves as a hammer to break this identification with the false "I." We then start realizing the Silence that has always existed even before the body came into being. We start knowing our true self, which is formless and limitless.

Human birth is indeed a grace. It attains true fulfillment only when we realize, "I am not the body" through direct experience, not just intellectually. Life is truly successful only when it is free from all beliefs and assumptions. "I am the body" is the root belief; all other beliefs arise from this root belief.

We cannot be completely free from sorrow as long as we mistake ourselves to be the body. **We attain true freedom only when we break free from this root belief of "I am the body." This freedom is Self-realization.**

Questions for Contemplation

- Contemplate your life and see how incidents have occurred to break your identification with the false "I" that you have assumed for yourself.

17

The Real I and the False I's

When we say, "I went to the market," "I am sitting," "I will go to the office," "I had food," we consider ourselves the body.

When we say, "I felt bad," "I am happy today," "I am getting bored," we assume ourselves the mind, as the body can never feel bad or bored.

When we say, "I thought," "I understood," "I disagree," we believe we are the intellect.

When we say, "Who am I? What is the purpose of my being on Earth?" the real I is speaking through the body. We need to know this real I not just intellectually, but through direct experience. When we realize this real I, it is the same as realizing God (Self, Pure Consciousness).

When we realize the real I, we see that the false I is merely a thought. This is the experience of Self-realization in which Silence is revealed to itself.

The false I is the ego, the persona, the costume. The real I is the Self, the Self-witnesser, the one who actually knows and experiences.

The real I wears the costumes of various false I's. The real I is the experience of living presence, which is ceaselessly going on. When we get deluded in the external world, we forget this real I; we are lost to this presence. We give undue importance to the false I, to the costume that we wear. To deepen our understanding of Silence, it is essential to remind ourselves of the difference between the real I and the false I's.

The real I – who-we-truly-are is our original nature. The false I is the costume, it is the ego which believes itself to be separate from others. If we clearly see who is speaking through our body and who-we-truly-are, then we won't get troubled or trapped in the dialogues of the false I. Instead, we will silently smile at it.

Throughout the day, we go about our activities with the false I. When we feel tired and fall asleep at the end of the day, the false I puts an end to itself. We cannot experience the bliss of deep sleep when the false I is active. When the real I alone remains, we fall asleep.

As soon as we wake up, the false I returns, as if it is saying, "I am back at your service. Together, let's take charge of everything." It seizes power and does not surrender to the truth of its falsity. It ruminates over all kinds of thoughts and does not quieten down even during meditation. At the end of the day, when the body gets tired, it wishes to be empty of thoughts, but that is not the case during daytime. Thus, the false I even tries to use sleep to its own advantage, without realizing that sleep happens only when it does not exist.

When life is flowing smoothly and happily without any hitch, the false I crafts problems of its own. ....
....

The false I thrives on conflict and disharmony. It feeds on acts of ridiculing, causing irritation, and fueling agitation. It gains strength from arguments and discord. We can imagine it as an angry mischievous child that makes fun of people, irritates them, beats someone up, abuses someone, or engages in fights. With these tendencies, the false I invites problems and then thrives on them.

The false I can accomplish everything except sleep and true relaxation. That is why it has to surrender and be quiet for sleep to occur.

With the practice of Silence, we need to awaken the real I so that it is not only experienced unconsciously in sleep but also consciously during the waking hours in the thick of activity. We also need to prepare the false I to surrender and be still even during the waking hours.

After waking up from sleep, when the false I eclipses the real I, the experience of the real I becomes feeble. In other words, the experience of the real I gets blurred in this eclipse. Actually, this experience remains the same at all times. It is changeless; it can never be feeble. It is always present as the silent awareness in the background of all the noise. However, due to the influence of the false I, the experience of the real I *appears* to be lost.

To always remember the real I, we need to ask ourselves, "Who am I now? A moment ago, I was playing some role, but who am I now?" This constant self-enquiry helps in undermining the influence of the false I's and revealing the real I.

Witnessing the real I in meditation

The practice of meditation helps in witnessing the real I. It leads to the awakening of the real I.

People all over the world practice various techniques of meditation and gain a variety of experiences. For example, many meditators make claims like, "I got such a profound experience in meditation today. I witnessed a brilliant light. I experienced such ethereal vibration. My body felt so light as if it was floating. I felt as if I was walking on the clouds," and so on.

Without knowing the real purpose of meditation, people remain stuck in the pursuit of such gross experiences. They consider these experiences as benchmarks for the success of their meditation practice. They believe that such experiences are signs of progress in their meditation.

The real purpose of meditation is that the real I should know itself. The one, who has worn this costume of the personality, should experience its true nature beyond all these costumes. It should emerge out of all such roles and know itself as the pure untouched knower of all experiences.

What will bring a truly hearty smile on our face? Playing the character in the drama of our worldly roles, or coming out of this drama? By being involved in this drama, we get trapped in the duality of pleasure and sorrow. A true smile can arise only when we emerge free from the drama of the various roles and abide as the real I. We need to practice meditation to develop recognition of the real I. When we realize the importance of this ultimate purpose, we will utilize the time we set aside for meditation to the fullest.

Meditation helps in the practice of Silence. The simple meaning of meditation is "doing nothing" or simply being present. But, for many people, "doing nothing" seems very difficult. In the first part of this book, we have seen that we don't have to do anything to sleep; we just have to lie down and be present. If we try hard to sleep, sleep eludes us.

In the same way, we don't need to do anything during meditation. We only need to be present. When we are only present, we become receptive to Silence. Then Silence reveals itself.

When we wake up from sleep, the first experience is that of Silence, devoid of thoughts, without the sense of body. The first thought that arises from Silence is the "I" thought. All other thoughts stem from the root "I" thought. Thus, the "I" thought is connected to all other thoughts on one side and to the Self on the other. Unless the "I" thought arises, no other thought can arise. Hence, it is essential to get to this root of all thoughts, which then reveals the thoughtless state of Silence.

When we consistently practice self-enquiry with the right understanding in every situation, or take time out in solitude to meditate on "Who am I?", the answer to "Who am I?" is revealed. This is because "Who am I?" is the first and foremost question. The answer is not an intellectual answer, but rather a direct experience of being the real I.

Until we entirely imbibe the understanding of Silence that this book points at, it will help to practice meditation every day. Just as clouds come and go in the sky, thoughts of the false I arise and subside during meditation. And when there are no thoughts, the cloudless sky of the real I is revealed. The real I is ever-present in the background. We will develop conviction in this truth through the practice of meditation. Only the real I will then prevail.

With consistent practice of meditation, we will not only become aware of the silence between two thoughts, but also of the thoughts arising between two intervals of silence. This will make it possible to experience Silence even in the midst of noise. We will be so deeply absorbed in Silence that meditation will happen effortlessly without the need to get rid of worldly noise. Despite being in the midst of noise, we can constantly abide in Silence.

When we realize the real I through direct experience in meditation, the thoughts that arise will be of bliss, devotion, veneration, expression of divine qualities, wonder, and divine service. These thoughts arise from Silence, because now only Silence prevails.

Regular practice of the following meditation can help in developing a clear recognition of Silence.

1. Before beginning, you may set a timer for ten minutes. You may use your mobile phone, a computer, a clock, or a watch for this.
2. Please close your eyes and sit in a comfortable posture.
3. Sit as if there is no future from now on. You do not have to go anywhere from here. You are here forever.
4. Had there been a future, you would be required to go somewhere. You would have to work, study, cook, feed your family. You would have done exercises. You would have prepared for festivals, shopped. But now, there is no future, and hence, there is none of this.
5. All there is, is right here, right now. This is the final truth. This moment in the now is the Truth.
6. You have locked the future. Now, nothing is going to happen. Only vast emptiness, Silence exists. You *are* this Silence.

7. You may perhaps find it difficult to abide in this Silence as the past is still present. Now, lock the past as well. Lock it in such a way as if nothing has ever happened before this moment. You are in this state since the beginning. This is the beginning and also the end.

8. Now, there is no food for the mind, only deep Silence. You are the Silence. You are the now.

9. If the mind tries to say something, remind it, "There is no future. Nothing at all is going to happen. There is no past. Nothing has ever happened." Just be aware of the Silence in the now.

10. You are liberated from the past and future. The mind has no role to play.

11. If nothing is going to happen, then there is no need to see anything. So, keep your eyes closed.

12. If you happen to hear any external sounds, ignore them. Be aware of this experience of Silent presence—the experience of Silence.

13. When the timer goes off, slowly open your eyes.

If you can stay without giving in to the mental pull of past and future, then you are always in Silence.

Questions for Contemplation

- What problems does the false I cause in your everyday life?
- What is the understanding with which you will practice meditation henceforth?

18

Walking with Faith on the Highway to Silence

There is a dense forest with many roads leading to different places. One of them is a highway that leads to a beautiful garden. Those who visit the forest wish to visit this garden but easily get confused and lose their way on the various roads that diverge from the highway. Despite their will, they fail to find their way to the highway. They keep going around the forest in circles, never reaching the garden.

This is exactly what happens with most of us in our spiritual life as well. We see many paths—some leading to Silence, and some misleading us away from Silence. We hear some people claiming that it is very difficult to attain the Truth in this very lifetime. Hence, we do not believe that we can ever attain the final truth that Saint Dnyaneshwar, Ramakrishna Paramhansa, Ramana Maharshi, Guru Nanak, and all other Self-realized souls attained. As a result, we get confused about the journey and give up, thus failing to attain the final truth.

To get out of this confused state, we first need unshakable faith on the way we are being guided in this journey. It is only with the arising of such faith that we can reach the state of Silence. Attaining this faith is not in our hands. The results that we experience in our life on this journey bring us the conviction that, "Yes! It is indeed true."

In this journey leading to the garden of Silence, we have now reached a point where we understand how our thoughts and emotions affect the experience of Silence.

As we practice meditation, listen to discourses on the Truth, and read literature on the Truth, our life undergoes a positive transformation, and our conviction on the Truth becomes stronger. We also develop faith in the certainty of reaching the garden of Silence while journeying through the dense forest of illusion.

By working on our thoughts and tendencies, we have reached this far on the journey of Silence. Silence reveals itself in our life based on the kind of faith that has arisen within us.

With the awakening of faith, we find ourselves on the highway. Hereafter, we need to keep walking straight ahead on this highway. No matter what, we need to stick to the highway and not stray away at any cost. When our faith falters, we begin to stray away from the highway. ....
....

As we walk on this highway, we will begin to sense some changes in the atmosphere. Even though we have not yet reached the garden of Silence, the breeze begins to carry its fragrance! The breeze that we sense has been through the garden of Silence. Hence, we begin to get wafts of its fragrance even while walking on the highway. The fragrance indicates that we are on the right track, strengthening our faith, thereby raising our conviction that we are on the right path.

While walking on this highway, day by day, we get even more convinced about who-we-truly-are and who-we-are-not. We have already received some indications about this from the previous chapters. As we progress through the further chapters and practice in earnest, we will also get liberated from attachment to our body and even the labels that we have fixated, such as, "I am a boy," "I am poor," "I am beautiful," etc.

Continue reading the book and practice the understanding to experience this eternal bliss. The further chapters will help us reach the garden where Silence is revealed in our life.

Questions for Contemplation

- How convinced are you of the certainty of reaching the garden of Silence?

NOTE

The chapters that follow provide a profound paradigm shift in the understanding of the Self. It will be helpful to pause at each sentence to reflect on the significance of what is being conveyed. When we pause and dwell in them, insight and clarity will emerge. It will also help to read these chapters a number of times to grasp their essence.

19

The Wondrous Game of the Self

The human body is non-living and insentient. Hence, it cannot get upset. Can a chair or a mike get upset? No. They are also non-living, non-aware objects. Therefore, they cannot get upset.

But still, when the body experiences pain, we say, "*I am* feeling pain. *I am* getting upset." Pain or fatigue happens with the body. But where does the pain or fatigue disappear during deep sleep? We experience no pain during deep sleep. In fact, we lose the sensation of the body in deep sleep.

When we get the thought, "I am unhappy," after all, who is unhappy? The non-living body cannot be unhappy, just as a chair cannot be unhappy. Can the mind be unhappy? What is the mind? The mind is nothing but a bundle of thoughts along with the root "I" thought.

Can a thought be unhappy? No, **a thought cannot be unhappy, though it may convey, "I am unhappy."**

> Suppose we are daydreaming of building a castle and appointing ten servants for its housekeeping. Suddenly, someone calls us, and we break out of our imagination of the castle. Do we lament about the shattered castle? No, we don't, because we know that it was not a real castle. It was just a thought about the castle.

In the same way, there is no separate individual who is unhappy. "I am unhappy" is just a thought, and the thought, by itself, is not unhappy. It carries information about an "I" that is supposed to be "unhappy." This is very subtle. The thought is not unhappy, but it carries an idea that "I am unhappy," and we become unhappy!

If neither the body nor the mind is unhappy, then is the Self unhappy? Can the Self—which is beyond all stories, all thoughts, and their content—ever be unhappy? Is the Self really unhappy, or is the Self having fun with such stray thoughts?

> It is like the king, who passes an order, and his people have to follow his order. For example, if the king says, "Trees are not green, they are black," his people quietly agree to him because the king has proclaimed it. He can proclaim anything and everything because he is the king. All his orders are followed.

In the same way, the Self is the supreme king. When the Self proclaims, "I am unhappy," the body agrees to it because the Self has declared it. The supreme king, who can never become unhappy, can announce, "I am unhappy," and the body will just trust it because the Self is saying so. Then the next day, the Self proclaims, "I am happy." The body trusts that too because the Self can say anything that it wishes.

The truth is, no one is unhappy or upset. The Self is using the medium of thoughts to declare anything it wishes and having fun. ....
....

> You may have seen a ventriloquist—one who performs shows where he throws his voice into a puppet to create an illusion as if the puppet is speaking. He plays the drama through the puppet. He throws words into the puppet and says, "I am the king." He can say anything through the puppet. To those who are observing, it appears as if the puppet is speaking.
>
> For example, the puppet may say, "I am really worried. I have lost my sleep. If the third world war starts tomorrow, what will happen to me?"
>
> What will you tell the puppet? You will say, "First, find whether you really exist." The puppet may continue with its blabber; it may say anything. But you won't take it seriously and you will allow it to play out. You know that it is non-living.
>
> The source of the puppet's words is elsewhere. When the puppet says, "I am very happy," you know *who* is actually happy. Whatever it says are the words of the ventriloquist.

In much the same way, whatever the body says are the thoughts created by the Self. Sometimes the body says, "I am happy," and at other times, it says, "I am unhappy." When we understand this game, we realize that what the body says is not actually true; it is just the content of thoughts that arise from the Self. **When we are firmly convinced that we are the Self, then thoughts cannot make us unhappy, even though they declare, "I am unhappy."**

Now, we need to detach ourselves from the body and shift to the Self. But thoughts cannot arise without the body. It doesn't matter whether the body is of dark or fair complexion, short or tall, fat or thin. It is important that the body must be alive. Hence, a variety of bodies are created by the Self; just one puppet won't suffice.

In the case of the ventriloquist's show, he says positive words through one puppet and negative words through another. The human body expresses a mix of both positive and negative thoughts. Every thought conveys the understanding of, "Who is the individual? Where is the individual? Actually who is unhappy? And who am I assuming to be unhappy?"

These doubts or questions are auspicious as they are seeds that break the attachment to thoughts, and ultimately to the "I" thought. These seeds arise from understanding. With practice, enquiring into each thought will become automatic. On every thought that occurs, we will immediately remember, "Who is actually thinking?" If we feel unhappy, we will question, "Who, really, is unhappy?"

The body is non-living by itself; it appears to be alive due to the presence of the Self. Thus, the body cannot be unhappy. But then, actually what is the "body?"

> **Consider a table on which we keep things. We call it a table, but is it actually a table? "Table" is just a label given to a form. Thus, "table" is a thought that arises when we see the thing that it represents.**

In the same way, "body" is also a label that arises as thought. Since childhood, we have been told that we are the "body." Hence, we have held on to this thought. In Chapter 3, we saw how the Buddha had questioned the disciple regarding the truth of "green" color. In much the same way, had we been told in childhood that it is a "pillar," what would it then be?

If we go deeper, we find that everything is the content of thoughts. The Self is untouched by the content of thoughts—whether they convey happiness or unhappiness. Then who is unhappy?

The Self alone witnesses all thoughts, and it is the Self who creates them too because it wishes to know itself using the medium of these thoughts. It wishes to sense its own presence using these thoughts as a sensing-mechanism. Rather than knowing the content of thoughts, the Self is actually interested in knowing itself. Whatever be the thought, the Self just wants to know itself.

> Whether we write, "I am happy," or "I am unhappy" on a glass surface, it doesn't matter to the glass. Both these sentences only convey the presence of the glass. Whether we write, "There is no glass here," or "There is a glass surface here," it only means the glass exists.

This means the Self can sense its own existence using the pretext of negative thoughts too. Every thought is actually conveying the presence of the knower of that thought.

Thoughts arise incessantly. We are witnessing them. If we know the place from where thoughts are being witnessed and get rooted therein, then we become stable.

When thoughts arise and knowing happens, then true witnessing of thoughts happens. **When a thought is known *after* it has occurred, then this is not true knowing. This is yet another thought that says, "This was a thought." This is merely the recalling from memory.**

Thoughts are arising and their knowing is happening. We need to stabilize in the experience of knowing. Then the sense of being a separate individual or ego will drop. This is called Self-realization. No individual can be Self-realized; no individual has ever realized the Self. When the separate "I" or ego vanishes, then realization happens, and the source of Silence is revealed to itself through that body-mind.

Questions for Contemplation

- How convinced are you that the separate individual is merely a figment of thoughts?
- How convinced are you that you are beyond thoughts?

20

Knowing without a Knower

When the Self associates with the body, the body comes alive. The body is non-living and insentient. Then actually, who are we?

We cannot be the non-living body as we are knowing whatever is happening around us. We experience being awake and aware. We may doubt the presence of everything, but how can we doubt the existence of our very own living presence that is knowing everything? Even to deny anything, a knower has to exist. This knower is not a know*er* as such, but a know*ing*, a witnessing presence.

The mind cannot grasp that there can be know*ing* without a know*er*... an action without an actor... a dance without a dancer. This know*ing* transcends the domain of the mind. All topics that belong to the mind's domain are based on words.

There is a noun and a verb for everything. There is a doer for every action. There has to be a dreamer for dreaming. This is due to the constraints of language. But actually there is no know*er*. There is only know*ing*; witnessing is happening.

Where dreaming happens, the dream alone exists without a separate dreamer. Similarly, where knowing is happening, knowing alone happens without a separate knower (the mind). ....
....

This know*ing* is the sense of "I am*ness*," the sense of beingness. It doesn't exist *in* the body. But as we have got the body, just like all other bodily experiences, we wish to experience this sense of beingness *in* the body. We wish that the body should experience this sense of beingness.

> It is like wearing a watch. We can clearly sense ourselves as being separate from the watch. We know that we are not the watch.

In this case, our body is like the watch. Our mind is a part of this watch. The mind wishes to check the experience of the Self.

> After wearing eyeglasses, we can see the outside world through them. But what if the eyeglasses insist on seeing us?! They can't.

Similarly, the mind cannot know the knower. But the mind keeps checking, "Let me see the Self. Let me know the Self. Let me see how this experience is." Despite all effort, the mind can never know the Self. But its effort of trying to know is also being witnessed. Let us understand this with an analogy.

> There is a house with a vent in the roof that lets in skylight. A person is sitting inside the house. He feels that no one outside knows whatever he does inside

the house. The truth is that he is being watched from outside through the vent. Whatever is going on inside the house is being known from outside.

When the person comes to know that whatever he does inside is being known outside, he feels, "I should get to know the one who is outside." Now, he strains his neck and tries to get a glimpse of the one who is outside.

Whether this person can succeed is another matter. But the one who is ever-present outside can see this person trying to crane his neck to look out from inside the house. In other words, the one who is trying to watch is being watched. The one who is trying to know is being known.

The mind needs to realize that its very attempt to know the Self is also being known. It is a hurdle in the experience of the Self. **This attempt of the mind is similar to an ignorant person trying to *see* music with his eyes.** We cannot use our eyes to see something which is not related to vision. In the same way, it is meaningless for the mind or thought to try to know the Self.

Know*ing* is outside the mind's domain. Whether the mind believes it or not, everything it does is being known. With understanding, the mind gets convinced about this and stops checking for this experience. When the mind surrenders, the ever-present Self is revealed to itself.

As we are attached to the body and firmly believe that "I am the body," we feel that "I am being watched." But when we realize through direct experience that we are neither the body nor the mind, then we shift out of the house, out of the body-mind. We gain the insight that we are always outside the house but believed we were inside.

We have always been *beyond* the body and mind but believed we *are* the body-mind.

Then the question arises: If we are outside the house, is there a need to know ourselves? Is there a need for the witnesser to witness itself?

As the body is present, the witnesser is knowing the body. It is also knowing the thoughts that are passing through the body. But why should the witnesser know itself?

To be able to know itself, it will have to divide itself into two—the knower and the known. But if the knower is separate from the known, then who will know the final knower? Let us understand this paradox with the help of an analogy.

> When we watch a movie on a screen, we cannot see the camera that has shot the scene. If we want to see that camera, we need a second camera to shoot the entire scene together with the first camera. This second camera won't be visible on the screen. Thus, the final camera can never be shown on the screen. It will always remain hidden.
>
> But while we watch the scene on the screen, we can sense the presence of this hidden camera due to which the scene exists, without which the scene can never be.

Similarly, whatever is happening in the realm of the mind is being witnessed from outside it. It is the final camera. Be convinced that the final witnesser cannot be known by standing apart from it. **We cannot *know* that; we can only *be* that because we already *are* that. Self alone exists. It doesn't need to know itself.**

As the mind gains conviction about this, it begins to surrender. Instead of insisting on knowing the Self, it becomes still. It realizes, "My role is not to know, but to move out of the picture." The mind's desire of knowing the Self dissolves. In other words, the Self stops getting the thought of knowing itself. Thereafter, it will be as if thoughts have stopped arising. Even if they do arise, they will only serve as a mirror for the Self to experience itself.

The absence of thoughts doesn't mean the absence of the Self. The Self exists even when there are no thoughts, experiencing its presence in Silence.

This is the most profound truth, which becomes clear only when we dwell in it. When we live in the essence of what is being said, insight will emerge. With understanding, such moments of clear insight will gradually increase. The mind remains immersed in a surrendered state. Detaching from the mind and dwelling in Silence becomes effortless.

Questions for Contemplation

- How prepared is your mind to surrender?
- Is there still a desire to know the Self, or is there the experience of being the Self?

PART 5
HOW TO EXPERIENCE SILENCE

In the journey of Silence, as we gain more understanding, even a momentary experience of Silence helps in developing a firm conviction and immense faith. The deeper understanding of the truth helps in abiding in Silence all the more. While walking, sitting, and performing all chores, we dwell in Silence.

We feel that Silence is revealed when thoughts stop arising or when there is a gap between thoughts. But it's not so. Silence is always present. It is the background on which thoughts occur. Thoughts arise from Silence and dissolve in it.

When Silence is experienced, we have only shifted our attention from the foreground noise to the background Silence. Thereafter, we watch every incident being in Silence.

21

The Sense of Beingness

When we are in Silence, we can clearly sense our beingness—the feeling of being alive. Beingness is the experience of the real "I," the Self. This experience transcends all bodily experiences.

When we stay in the experience of beingness, we are not affected by what people say. For example, if someone says, "Oh no! Such a bad thing happened to you. You were insulted," we will clearly spot the false "I" to which this story belongs and remain in our beingness without getting stuck in the trap of the story.

Let us conduct the following experiment to experience beingness.

Please close your eyes and sit in silence for some time.

1. Imagine that your entire body has changed. You have received an entirely new body with a new face.
2. Just watch yourself being in that body.
3. How is your sense of beingness? How is your feeling of being alive? Has it changed due to change in the body, or does it remain the same?
4. You will clearly experience that your beingness is still the same. Your feeling of aliveness has not changed with change in the body.
5. Slowly open your eyes.

You would have experienced that despite changing your body, your beingness remains the same. This means the sense of beingness is beyond the body. It has nothing to do with the body. But we keep trying to seek that experience in the physical body.

Did you need to think about beingness to experience it? Not at all! You just needed to *be* it. Experiencing beingness is so simple.

We mostly value whatever is physically visible. We usually give a lot of importance to the tangible experiences that we physically sense. Sensory inputs viz. sights for the eyes, tastes for the tongue, touch for the skin, smell for the nose, and sounds for the ear, overpower us. Hence, the experience of beingness gets shrouded.

There is a difference between the experience of beingness and what we experience through our senses. What we perceive through our senses is an illusion because it is subject to interpretation by the mind. Yet, we value it more than the experience of beingness.

The essential thing that needs to be valued is beingness; it is intangible. It is the only truth. We cannot perceive beingness through physical senses; we can experience it only in Silence. When we sense beingness through direct experience, then life becomes simple and straightforward. Until then, we continue to give all importance to bodily experiences only.

The sense of beingness is not in the body; it transcends the body. However, the mind believes it to be in the body and keeps searching for it. It then declares that it had got this experience once and has now lost it. However, it's not so. The mind's imagination and beliefs are a hurdle in the experience of beingness.

Just like the hands of the clock incessantly keep ticking without a break, the experience of beingness is also continuously going on. It has never stopped, nor will it ever end. Had it stopped even for a fraction of a second, we could have grasped it easily because of its momentary absence.

We can dive into the ocean and also come out on the shore. Hence, we can grasp the experience of the ocean as we can stand apart from it on the shore. But the same thing is not possible with the experience of beingness. We cannot get out of the experience of beingness because it is beyond the concepts of "inside" and "outside." Everything arises inside this experience of being alive. Therefore, it can be experienced only by *being* it.

We try to compare beingness with what we perceive through our physical senses. But this comparison leads us away from that experience. The experience of beingness is different from that of time, space, age, and other aspects.

The truth of the calendar

The calendar shows us our age, and we undoubtingly believe it. If we calculate the days, months, and years since our birth by referring to the calendar, we may feel that we have lived a long life. But the experience of beingness is entirely different.

This anomaly also happens in dreams. When we are into the dream, we feel that the dream is going on for a long duration. But when we wake up, we remember it as something that lasted only for a short time. ....
....

While being in the dream, we have never asked ourselves, "How long is this dream going on?" It is only after we wake up from the dream that we realize whether the dream was short or long.

Similarly, we use the calendar to measure the length of our life. But when we see it without any means of measurement, we don't feel we have lived as long as what the calendar shows us. The calendar cannot give us the right measure of our age in experiential terms.

The truth of people

Since our childhood, parents, relatives, and neighbors have unanimously told us, "You are a boy. You are a girl," and we have assumed this to be true. All these statements ultimately tell us only one thing—"You are the body." And we firmly believe it.

We make our decisions based on whatever we have learned since childhood. We have more faith in our beliefs than what our experience of beingness tells us. What we perceive from beingness is altogether different from what our physical senses convey. But we always tend to believe whatever the physical senses say.

The truth of time

The clock measures the passage of time. It reports that we have worked for eight hours from morning till evening. But while we were busy at work, did we realize the quantum of time that has passed? Without referring to the clock, how long do we feel we have worked based on our experience of beingness? If we ponder such questions, we will recognize the fallacy of measured time.

When we love what we are doing, we are completely engrossed in it and lose the sense of time. Each hour seems to fly by in a minute. In this way, we can work for long hours without realizing that we have worked for so long. On the contrary, when we are doing something boring to the mind, each minute seems to drag like an hour.

Just because we trust our clocks more than our own experience, we don't easily trust the truth: **We are ageless and timeless.**

We should not forget the experiential truth in our attempt to rationalize everything in logical terms, .

If time is the truth, then just consider—

- Why do we feel that time has flashed by so quickly when we are happy?
- When we have to prepare for our exams overnight, why does time seem to scuttle by without our realizing it?
- When we are eagerly waiting for someone, why does every minute seem like an hour?

Whether time has passed quickly or slowly, the experience of the Self remains the same. That experience never changes.

Contemplating these questions will bring us the realization that time is not real. This realization will take us closer to the experience of the Self. Since time is not the truth, it doesn't matter whether we experience it or not. In the same way, it doesn't matter whether we experience our age or not. Of course, we will use common sense to make use of time effectively to fulfill our roles in the world.

But if we are making the mistake of ignoring the experience of beingness, we need to be aware of it. We *are* beingness; we are the Self. Now, let the Self experience its timeless presence through the body-mind. Let the Self operate from beingness and perform all actions from that standpoint.

Questions for Contemplation

- How old do you feel in terms of your experience?
- What hurdles do you experience in living from the standpoint of beingness?

22

Zero is Positive

When we operate in the domain of the mind, we believe in worldly definitions of success. These beliefs drive our entire life. We may pursue various worldly goals and become successful in worldly terms. We may fulfill all our desires, attain fame and prosperity. But we continue to feel a void within. We don't feel complete and contented.

In an attempt to fulfill this urge for completeness, we constantly engage in one pursuit after another till the very end of our life. In such a life, we find ourselves enmeshed in the constant flux of desires. Our mind remains overtly active. Our body also gets programmed with such habits and patterns of behavior.

Living such a life is like living in a dream. We may be living in the midst of luxuries, but far from being who-we-truly-are. If we want to wake up from this dream of being a limited individual, we need to be who we are—the limitless Self.

Once we wake up from this endless dream of worldly pursuits, we will dwell in the eternal bliss and contentment of the Self. Whether we have any material comforts or we don't, it won't really matter to us. Even if we do get these material possessions, we will put them to appropriate use for the experience and expression of the Self; we won't chase after them. Such a life is indeed successful—a life wherein we are free from the traps of the mind and body, and dwell in beingness.

When we are operating from the domain of the mind, we may think, "What will happen to me? What about my future?" On the other hand, when we operate from the sense of beingness, we get the thought, "Who am I?" All these are thoughts, but the key point is—which thought will lead us closer to the experience of the Self?

> **Suppose two friends, Jay and Vijay, are stationed at Pune. Both are dreaming that they are at Lonavala (midway between Pune and Mumbai). In his dream, Jay is traveling towards Pune. Vijay is travelling in the other direction towards Mumbai in his dream. Their goal is to reach Pune.**

Whose dream is better? You might say, "After all, both are dreams and are bound to break." But the dream that leads Vijay to Mumbai could delude him throughout his dream life. In Jay's dream, as he is traveling towards Pune, he has the likelihood of reaching Pune someday, where he can emerge from his dream and open his eyes. This is the secret of breaking of the dream.

When one is in a dream, he is everywhere else, except his original place. In the dream, if he were to return to his original place where he actually is, then he could immediately wake up.

In the above analogy, traveling towards Pune symbolizes moving towards Silence with clarity, whereas traveling towards

Mumbai indicates moving away from Silence towards worldly entanglement in confusion.

There are very few exceptional cases where people could break out of their dream while moving into worldly entanglement. But we need to consider the law of averages to assess the kind of thoughts (dreams) that occur for one to shift to Self-realization (waking up).

To understand which dream is better, we need to understand the final thought that occurs just before Self-realization. How much does the Self delay by holding onto thoughts before Self-realization? For example, if the Self is obsessed with the thought, "I want to experience the Self, but I cannot." How much does the Self delay having the final thought in that body? The final thought that emerges could probably be, "Oh! This is just another thought!" This final thought could arise earlier in some bodies, and later in others. Such variations do happen. But there is nothing like "early" or "late," "good," or "bad" about it from the Self's point of view.

The important point is to know the kind of thoughts that are currently passing through our body. If they are leading us towards the experience of the Self, then we are moving towards clarity (Pune, in the analogy). With clarity, the final thought could occur any moment, leading to awakening from the dream.

However, if the thoughts are pertaining to the domain of the mind, then we are drifting away towards worldly entanglement (Mumbai, in the analogy). In this case, we need to stop immediately in our tracks. The sooner we stop, the less farther we move away from clarity.

Stopping here doesn't mean that we have stopped making progress. On the contrary, the stopping helps us change the direction of our journey towards clarity and awakening. Thus, not progressing further proves to be real progress in the longer run.

> On a numerical scale, when we are moving from negative to positive, we need to cross zero. When we reach zero, we may feel as if we have stopped making progress. It is vital to remind ourselves that we were in negativity and are now moving towards positivity. Positivity starts only after reaching zero. When we look at it from negativity, reaching zero is a positive move.

Similarly, when we are mired in worldly entanglements, we need to first stop thinking in that direction. When we stop entertaining worldly thoughts, it may appear as if we have stopped making worldly progress. But, if this pause is helping us shift towards neutral thoughts (zero) and then move towards positive thoughts that eventually lead to thoughts of the Truth, then it is a sign of real progress.

We need to start inculcating thoughts of the Truth that will help in dwelling in the experience of the Self. These thoughts of Truth will lead to the occurrence of the final thought before Self-realization. This final thought alone can awaken us from our stupor into the experience of the Self.

Given this possibility, if we are turning back from negativity towards positivity and clarity, isn't reaching zero auspicious?!

Questions for Contemplation

- In which direction are your thoughts leading you today—entanglement or clarity?
- How intense is your desire to awaken from this dream?

23

Self-Experience with Right Understanding

The experience of the Self pervades and transcends all situations. It is the same in the past, present, and the future. It is the same in all seasons, places, in living and non-living beings. It is the same, regardless of religious beliefs. It is the same in each and every one.

If the Self alone exists, then how can it experience and express itself? Let us understand this with the help of an analogy.

> If the tongue has to experience itself, it has to divide itself into two—that which tastes, and that which is tasted.

Similarly, the Self needs to divide itself into two for experiencing itself. The Self has manifested itself as all the beings of the universe. Thus, the body-mind mechanisms are numerous and different, but the experience of the Self is the same in all of them.

Self-to-Self talk is going on—the Self is talking to itself through multiple body-minds. It experiences itself through all human bodies consciously or unconsciously, whether the body-mind has a quest to attain the experience of the Self or not.

To extend this game further and derive bliss, the Self has forgotten "Who am I" and believes itself to be the individual body. After getting entangled in the drama of the world, it again seeks its true nature. **Isn't this the greatest comedy—forgetting and then trying to remember oneself, when one is already what one is seeking!**

The sense of beingness is there in all body-minds. But due to lack of right understanding, the seeking remains an insatiable pursuit. People adopt various practices in spirituality. Some chant mantras, while some perform other rituals. Some visit various places to gain mystical experiences. Some go on pilgrimage, some visit temples, some take to the mountains, while some experience ethereal vibrations in their meditations. All of them are meant for realizing the experience of the Self—the sense of beingness.

Having experienced this state, one says, "I was in that state for an hour. I didn't feel like talking to anyone for the next couple of hours. I was immersed in Silence. However, everything came back to normal after three to four hours."

This implies that they have not gained any understanding. They may have experienced the sense of beingness, but their understanding remains the same as they lack a firm conviction of the experience. Without the right understanding, they return to square-one despite these experiences. No matter how prolonged or successful their experience may have been, they experience a feeling of void and lead a dissatisfied life of a limited individual. Instead, if they had sat in Silence with the right understanding only for a minute, it would have made a huge difference.

When the right understanding emerges, the beliefs, "I am the body, I am the experiencer, I am the doer," begin to break. We learn to detach from the body and abide in beingness. The eureka can then occur any time as the experience of the Self is ceaselessly going on. Even glimpses of this experience bring a big leap in our understanding, and our behavior changes.

Earlier, we were leading life based on the belief that we are the individual body-mind. We were functioning based on the beliefs of our body-mind. Despite trying hard, we were not able to come out of the traps of the mind. But as we return to our true identity—the Self—we break out of this mechanical way of living and begin to lead an intuitive, spontaneous, and fresh life.

Realizing the experience of the Self should be given the topmost priority in our life. But society is structured on such beliefs that most people do not have Self-experience on their life of priorities. The illusory world has numerous avenues for false happiness. One hankers after all kinds of worldly pleasure. "Let me first watch my favorite program on TV; then I will meditate. Let me enjoy this tasty dish; then I will dip into the experience of beingness. Let me first play this game on my mobile phone; then I will take some time for meditation," and so on. One leads life based on the experiences that belong in the mind's domain.

Self-experience is not for the mind

In an attempt to know the knower, the doubting mind keeps raising questions and doubts about Self-experience. "If experiencing the Self is so easy, then why am I unable to grasp it?" This question may seem logically right. But the paradox here is that the doubting mind, which is trying to experience the Self has to be convinced that it can never attain that experience.

"Why am I unable to grasp the experience of the Self?" is just another thought that is passing before you. You are witnessing it by being in the experience of the Self. The thought wants to grasp the experience of the Self. You need to counter-question this thought, "First, tell me why you need to grasp the experience of the Self?" Recognize this thought that is trying to send you away in search of yourself! Watch this thought as just a thought. Then another thought will arise, "There is no need to grasp the experience of the Self." This thought will cut the first thought and you will then abide in the experience of the Self. Your very presence is Self-experience in itself, which transcends all thoughts. Hence, there is no need to grasp any thought for seeking the Self...................
....

With this understanding, all thoughts about seeking the Self cease. Then only Self-awareness remains. The game of seeking comes to an end. But then, the Self can extend this game by giving another thought, "The experience is already there. I can know it anytime. I can enjoy it any time. Let me first know some other interesting things."

Thus, most people are stuck in pursuing everything else, except being in Self-experience. If we already possess something, it is but natural for us to say, "As I already have it, I can enjoy it any time later. Let me first experience something else right now." Keeping aside the very purpose of Self-experience for which we are alive, we get entangled in everything else in the world.

Hence, it is essential to understand the experience of the Self. In other words, the mind should realize that it cannot grasp this experience. When we become free from the whims of the mind and learn to abide in Self-experience, our life becomes simple and brims with pure joy and playfulness.

Questions for Contemplation

- What are the thoughts that the Self is holding onto in your body-mind mechanism?

24

The State of Complete Surrender

At the final milestone on this journey of Silence, people believe that they just need to be in meditation. They feel they don't need to react to any situation. They just need to be silent and give up on everything. They consider not correcting anything or anyone as the act of giving up everything.

However, this attitude still entangles them in the mind's trap as the mind still has some role to play in it. It checks whether we are precisely following what is being told and tries to ensure that the so-called "ideal" state is maintained. It also takes credit for attaining and staying in this "ideal" state. But as soon as the mind tries to be in control, Silence gets obscured.

The secret is to be open. Neither hold onto doing, nor refrain from doing. Neither give up nor hold onto anything. Neither this, nor that.

When we try to fixate and hold onto one side of any aspect, we are not completely open. When we are open, we understand a new way of responding to people and situations without fixating anything. The mind would insist on knowing exactly what is to be done. It is comfortable when a clear list of do's and don'ts is defined. It experiences discomfort when it is not sure of what is to be done.

"Neither this nor that," what kind of response is this? What does it mean to be open and not anticipate any fixed outcome?

It is like we have given up applying effort from our side, and everything is happening intuitively and spontaneously in a free flow. Thoughts do not block the flow. We see creations smoothly and harmoniously manifesting in our life when the individual "I" has surrendered to the flow of life.

Let us understand it with the help of an example.

> When Jesus was crucified, his body was enduring excruciating pain. But his mind completely surrendered to the divine will, and he bided through the crucifixion with the thought, "Let Thy will be mine."

Complete surrender can happen in daily life situations as well.

> Consider someone who is facing a situation where all the parts of his body are experiencing severe pain. But he thinks, "This painful period is preparing me for something grand." With such a thought, a state of complete surrender emerges in his body. By giving supreme importance to the divine will, his body plays to the divine tune.

This can happen with everyone, but not everyone realizes it because such glimpses are rare. We need to grasp the essence of Silence to make these glimpses an everyday experience. When one enters this state, one sees things miraculously unfolding in their life.

> It is like we are playing the piano, and the music that is played gets scripted on paper. It is as if we are typing it on paper. If this could happen, then composing music would be so easy!

In life, our body-mind is the piano. But when the truth dawns on us, we realize that **we are not playing the piano; instead, we are being played! The body-mind is being played by divine will.**

Close your eyes for a moment and imagine that your body-mind is the piano. Experience your body-mind being played. After some time, open your eyes and continue reading.

....

Our body-mind can be played by the Self only when our ego completely surrenders. Everything then starts appearing in our life intuitively and spontaneously. This is an indication that divine expression is happening in our life. Seeing this expression, we will be filled with wonder because it would exceed all our hopes and expectations.

When people see a Self-realized Guru delivering a discourse, they believe that *he* has delivered the discourse. But in reality, the discourse emerges from Silence, and the Guru's body serves as a medium for its expression.

We are familiar with the language of "doing." The language of "being done, being played" is unknown to most people.

When we understand the essence of Silence, we don't play, but *we are played*. We serve as instruments for the divine expression of Silence.

When we are operated from Silence, the right response emerges naturally. If we understand this thoroughly, our life will become simple and spontaneous. It will become easier to experience the bliss of Silence every moment. Responses that arise from Silence are fresh and novel, bringing about a complete change in our expression.

Complete surrender is a simple secret that anyone can understand. Having understood it, we will experience that actions are being enacted through the body, and everything is unfolding in our life spontaneously. **We only need to realize that there is no doer. Every scene unfolds as a part of happening.**

When the human body is being played, then the highest wisdom emerges through it intuitively. The highest scriptures, divine hymns, poetry, profound analogies, soulful music get composed through it. Various forms of service are rendered through it. These highest forms of expression manifest only upon complete surrender of these bodies to the divine play (*Leela*). Some people are touched by such expression so profoundly that the state of surrender intuitively arises within them. We need to experience this happening with us.

For this to happen, we have to consciously remember and abide in this state initially. Later, it will happen on its own. We will find that the body is present in a receptive and empty state, and it is being played without any sense of doer-ship in the body. ....
....

Complete Surrender

> Imagine an idol of God made of jaggery. When it moves its hand on its belly, it catches hold of some jaggery. It makes a miniature idol out of this jaggery that it retrieves

from its own belly. This miniature idol represents a human being.

Just like all beings, we humans, too, are made out of God. But in ignorance, we consider ourselves separate from God.

Now, this separate human being worships God. He prays, "O God, I surrender everything to you. Nothing is mine." After his prayer, he pinches out some jaggery from the idol and offers it back to God. In this entire ritual, he believes, "I have surrendered everything to God." But what is he? He doesn't realize that he, too, has been formed from the same jaggery.

While surrendering to God or performing rituals, he doesn't realize even once, "*Who* is surrendering all of this?" The one who is offering tries to stand apart from what is offered. When he attains the right understanding, he realizes, "I am also part of the offering! I need to surrender myself too. Only then can complete surrender happen."

If he surrenders by safeguarding his ego (the false "I"), the surrender is not complete. Incomplete surrender doesn't bring about the merger into oneness. With complete surrender, he will stabilize in Silence.

Since ages, spiritual scriptures and doctrines have emphasized the importance of surrender. When we surrender completely, bliss is experienced. Thereafter, we revel in the timeless state of Silence, bliss, and love even during daily chores.

Questions for Contemplation

- How prepared is your body-mind for complete surrender so that the divine tune can play through it?

25

The Joy of Surrendering with Understanding

When a musician is fully absorbed in composing music, a masterpiece gets created. When the music is being composed, the musician is lost in it, as if he doesn't exist. He has become one with the composition.

Similarly, we also get totally absorbed while completing certain activities in our daily life. After these activities are completed, we can marvel at the creation and wonder, "Wow! I haven't done anything to come up with such a beautiful creation! Certainly, it just happened on its own."

The important question is: If this can happen for a short period of time, how can it pervade our entire life?

For some time, just imagine a life of complete surrender, where everything is happening on its own without any doer. It is like a piano that is constantly playing one melody after the other on its own. All activities happen spontaneously, and we don't feel that we are doing anything at all. All responses emerge from Silence, and there is no feeling of being separate from whatever is happening. Don't we feel elated even by imagining such a life?!

When there is complete surrender to the Self, the body is played spontaneously like a piano. However, if the body desires to do something on its own, then it poses a hurdle in surrendering. The ego wishes to fulfill its own desire under the pretext of aligning with the divine will. We need to understand the meaning of complete surrender to get rid of this.

With a deep understanding of complete surrender, acting upon this understanding and surrendering, both happen at the same time. Even if this has not happened for any of our unresolved problems, we can at least mentally tell ourselves, "Now, I have surrendered this problem to God (the Source, the Self, *Allah*, *Ishwar*, Consciousness)."

If someone asks, "What happened about your promotion?" "What happened about your job?" we can mentally tell ourselves, **"I have surrendered it to God."**

If we face some problem in completing a task, if it is getting delayed, then we will not consider it as a problem. Instead, we will completely surrender it to God.

Everything that we may ever need for a fulfilled life is waiting to manifest in our life. But it stops midway and does not manifest only because we are not prepared to surrender completely. We keep believing that we have to do everything on our own. The mind is not prepared to relinquish its need to be in control. It does not easily let go of the habit of taking credit for whatever happens. It does not keep all the ways open for things to occur

in life. The mind keeps us away from the truth and poses a hurdle in surrendering completely. ....
....

To overcome this hurdle, we need to develop the habit of surrendering all our problems to God. With this habit, the judging and comparing mind won't pose any hurdle in complete surrender. Complete surrender brings balance, harmony, and spontaneity, which leads to the experience of true happiness.

You will have to experiment with this to see it happening in your life. For example, take out some time every day to observe how everything is happening on its own. Watch how your body is being played, how responses emerge in various situations. This helps to transition from being a doer to being a seer. Then the bliss of pure awareness will be experienced. You will marvel in amazement, "Indeed... life is so beautiful; everything is happening like a song."

There is an abundance of love, bliss, and peace in everyone's life. But as one is not convinced that such a life is possible, one remains deprived of the utter joy that can be experienced in any situation—whether it is trivial or major. By abiding in complete surrender, we can be in the flow and enjoy each and every moment of life as it unfolds.

Questions for Contemplation

- How often do you experience Silence in your daily life? Is it increasing by the day?

26

The Art of Complete Surrender

When we learn any physical sport, we practice consistently to get better at it. We practice shadowboxing to overcome our errors and improve our game further. But when it comes to conquering our mind, we believe it is impossible. We are shaken by watching the exploits of our mind and wonder, "O God! How can I rein in my mind? It seems impossible to control it."

The answer to such questions lies in studying the mind. Such questions render the strength to undertake deep contemplation on the mind and study it thoroughly. Understanding Silence and the art of complete surrender makes this seemingly impossible endeavor possible. Let us understand this with the help of an example.

Most of the Martial Arts movies portray a very brave and powerful villain. No one seems to be able to defeat him. On the contrary, the hero is portrayed as a timid character. But then, the hero is prepared to learn and develop himself despite his weaknesses.

The villain tortures all the people, including the hero. When the hero loses his tolerance, he resolves to defeat the villain. He seeks guidance from a guru for this purpose. The guru teaches him how to fight the villain. He makes him undergo a strict regimen and rigorous training. Whenever the hero challenges the villain for a fight, he gets beaten up by the villain. Despite this, he continues his practice relentlessly under the able guidance of the guru.

Initially, whenever he faces problems, he tightens his belly. He stands in a constricted posture as he has been habituated to facing problems this way since his childhood. Then the guru repeatedly puts him on the right track and makes him learn the new way. He repeatedly tells the hero, "You can win only if you fight as you are told."

In the end, the guru imparts the final lesson, "You need to loosen your body and fight. Just relax and leave your body loose. You were tightening your body with the desire to win. Now let your body loose with the readiness to lose." So far, the hero was struggling to safeguard himself by resisting the blows of the villain. But now, the guru asks him to fight as if he is intoxicated by alcohol!

You would have seen how drunkards wobble randomly without resisting whatever comes their way. They even fall and get hurt badly but do not seem to be bothered. They rise again as if nothing has happened.

When the hero remembers this last lesson during his fight with the villain, he stops resisting the blows. Just like a drunkard, he lets his body loose, relaxes himself, and then fights. In the end, he triumphs.

Life is like such a movie. ....

....

The problems that we face in our everyday life are like the villain. Some problems weaken and dent us. But those who do not resist whatever comes, emerge winners like the hero in the movie. They overcome their weaknesses, develop the required skills, and then confront the problems. Such people don't fear problems and learn the art of dissolving them with complete acceptance. We also need to learn how to dissolve all the problems of our life. This is the art of complete surrender. To master this art, we need to practice being in Silence.

Loosening ourselves is no lesser than any fine art. If someone warns us in advance, "I am going to blow my fist on your belly," we will immediately cringe and tighten our belly first. When he actually blows his fist on the belly, we will face the least trouble as we are prepared for the blow.

This is what most people do when they face problems in life. As soon as a problem arises, they immediately constrict and tighten themselves and then go through the troublesome situation. This may seem to be an effective way of dealing with problems.

But the art of complete surrender is different. Instead of tightening ourselves, we just need to loosen ourselves and then endure the blow. This means we wholeheartedly face the biggest problems in our life with forbearance and understanding.

When we tighten in the context of life situations, we resist them. We believe that we can confront the situation by resisting it. On the other hand, loosening ourselves implies completely accepting the situation as-it-is by being in Silence. The complete acceptance that emerges from being in Silence is not a forceful compulsive acceptance. It is the acceptance that arises from a deep understanding. After attaining wisdom, we are freed from all compulsions. Acceptance becomes our nature.

Accepting problems out of compulsion is like a bounded labor. But with the art of complete surrender, it is not so. We will accept problems from a state of freedom and flow with the way life unfolds.

We need to flow through all situations of our life smoothly by loosening ourselves. Initially, we may feel discouraged at the idea of loosening ourselves to receive the blows of life's challenges. But with the power of complete acceptance, we can sail through life. The solutions to all our problems will then emerge from Silence.

Even if the problems are trivial, it helps to remember, "Let me be in Silence now and surrender completely. I will then watch how the solution unfolds naturally."

We need to consistently practice being in Silence every day to master this art of complete surrender. As we progress further, we will become so proficient in this fine art that it will become our nature.

Questions for Contemplation

- With the understanding gained from this chapter, how will you face challenging situations in life?

27

Being the Harmonium

As we practice being in Silence with complete surrender, we attain the timeless state of Silence—*Samadhi*. In this state, all our inner demons can be annihilated completely. But for that, we need to develop the habit of contemplation. Every incident in our life provides an opportunity for contemplation.

In today's digital age, people get all sorts of information at their fingertips. Hence, they don't feel the need to contemplate on their own. But it is essential to develop the habit of contemplation and bring self-discipline. If we happen to get any new information during daily chores, we need to take some time out to reflect on it and assess its real worth.

The mind may say, "Why do I need to contemplate when people are feeding me with readymade information?" We need to tell the mind, "I need to contemplate to assess whether it aligns with my ultimate purpose of living in complete surrender."

If contemplation has brought about a positive transformation in others' lives, then it can surely happen in our life too. Without contemplation, we will be shaken by the onslaught of life's challenges. If we keep reflecting on each and every incident in our life, then we are more likely to remember what we have learned when those incidents repeat in the future. This will prepare us to lead our life in complete surrender. With consistent reflection and practice of Silence, we gradually progress towards a thoughtless state; we become empty.

Nature fills empty bowls with the wisdom of Silence. Hence, we need to first empty our bowls! As we get rid of the ego and become empty, we are intuitively guided by nature. If we decode the guidance correctly, we can walk the path to our ultimate goal. The grime of the ego makes one unworthy of receiving such guidance.

Water never stays atop mountains; it naturally flows down towards the rivers to fill the empty space. The same law applies to humans as well. **This is the art of becoming empty. The one who is empty from within alone receives the water of Silence.**

There is a popular proverb: **A reed before the wind lives on, while mighty oaks do fall.** The oak tree trusts in its own strength to withstand the storm and is blown over, while the reed that bends and sways with the wind survives and thrives because it surrenders.

Just like the reed calmly surrenders to the windstorm, we too need to surrender ourselves to the flow of life. The stubborn oak tree of the ego gets torn down. This is the importance of complete surrender and becoming empty.

When the witnesser becomes empty of all inclinations and tendencies, the Self-witnesser (Silence) is revealed.

....

Body-mind as a Harmonium

As we completely surrender to the divine will, our body-mind becomes like a harmonium. We no longer try to control any situation or people. We go beyond wins and losses, and flow with the way nature intuitively guides. The harmonium starts playing to the tune of the Self from morning till night.

As we get up in the morning, our harmonium will start humming the song of beingness—the hum of "Am-ness." We become like a child who enjoys watching everything for the first time. We will keep humming wherever possible, using common sense to avoid doing it where it is not possible. Otherwise, people may wonder, "What's wrong with you?"

> Animals lead a natural and spontaneous life. They are not bothered about what will happen next. If they are inside water, it is as if they have *become* water. When they get out of water, they simply jerk off the water and proceed with whatever comes next. They act like a harmonium—completely in harmony with nature.

But the same doesn't immediately become possible with humans because we don't remember to live this way. We are habituated to tighten and cringe, trying to control whatever is happening. If things don't happen as per our will, we become angry and hateful. But as a harmonium, we need to relax ourselves and watch with wonder how everything happens beautifully.

> If we are waiting in a queue, instead of becoming impatient, we will patiently wait and watch with wonder for our turn. Until then, we will keep humming. Thus,

waiting in a queue will also become an "online" spiritual practice.

Suppose we are waiting for someone to complete certain tasks and they haven't done it. By habit, we will become angry, but as a harmonium, we will relax.

For ages, all activities are ceaselessly happening on Earth. Nothing has stopped. The list of activities is never-ending. As our body-mind plays like a harmonium, instead of tightening, we watch how every activity gets completed in a relaxed manner. There is a harmony and rhythm to everything.

We need to learn this art of relaxed functioning like a harmonium, where we are in complete harmony with nature, dancing to the tune of the Self, humming the song of "being alive" and witnessing things getting completed in the best possible way. If we face any problem, we simply place it in the harmonium and see how it gets resolved on its own.

If we start living this way, we become a relaxed magnet that attracts the best for the wellbeing of all beings. Our body-mind becomes instrumental for the experience and expression of Silence in a true sense.

Questions for Contemplation
- How will you develop the habit of contemplation?
- How prepared are you to flow with the way life unfolds spontaneously?

28

The Practice of Samadhi

We have been practicing being in the waking, dream, and deep sleep states during our daily life cycle. But, unless we practice being in Silence, the cycle doesn't get completed.

> It is as if we are riding a bicycle and have forgotten the parcel kept on its carrier. That parcel is the discovery of our true nature.

If we do everything else in life except knowing who-we-truly-are, we have forgotten the most important thing for which we are here on Earth. This parcel can be uncovered only when we dwell in Silence. Hence, we need to make arrangements to make meditation an integral part of our daily routine.

When we successfully practice sleeping, dreaming, being in the waking state, and being in the timeless state of Silence, then we transcend these four states and attain the fifth state beyond these four. This fifth state is called the *Turiya-ateet* state (the state beyond the fourth) or *Sahaj Samadhi* (the state of being in Silence while acting in the world). **The ultimate goal of life is to attain Sahaj Samadhi while the physical body is alive.**

To attain this state, we need to first start with *Savikalp* Samadhi, wherein we take the support of some pretext or ritual for being in Silence. For example, the breath can be used as a pretext to shift into Silence. Chanting can be used as a ritual to shift into Silence. Initially, people don't understand what they should do in meditation. They believe that closing their eyes and sitting in a yogic posture means being in Samadhi. But it's not so.

Until the experience of the Self is known through direct experience, we need to practice Savikalp Samadhi. Gradually we learn to witness the rise and fall of thoughts and begin to sense the witnesser of all thoughts. The witnesser has many topics and things to witness in the world. But as the number of thoughts reduces, the witnesser becomes aware of its own presence and becomes the Self-witnesser. Then we experience *Nirvikalp* Samadhi.

In the state of Nirvikalp Samadhi, all delusion vanishes, and Silence experiences itself. This state is called Self-experience, Beingness, Pure consciousness, Bright Silence, the sense of being alive, or Self-in-rest. In this timeless state of Silence, the answer to "Who am I?" is experienced, leading to a firm conviction in it. The body shifts from the mode of "doing" and calms down into the state of "being." There are no thoughts. The thoughts that try to check or judge the experience vanish, and so do the thoughts that take credit for the experience. The body is stable in a peaceful and relaxed state. The breath keeps flowing in and out steadily. There is complete acceptance and surrender.

The desire of doing something in the world arouses the ego within us, whereas the state of complete surrender in Silence eliminates the ego.

We become one with nature. We marvel at this divine play of nature and abide in the feelings of love, bliss, peace, veneration, and amazement. We remain relaxed and wonder at the spontaneity of all the happenings of the world. We experience a feeling of natural flow in everything, which is an indication that we are in the state of complete surrender.

On the contrary, when we try to fixate or force-fit something in our life, when we try to convince others to act as per our wishes, then we should immediately realize, "I am trying to apply force. This means I am not in the state of complete surrender."

In the state of complete surrender, we have to do nothing. We just need to be in the flow of the way life unfolds spontaneously. This is not something ordinary. It takes remarkable daring to "do nothing." Those who have learnt the art of being empty alone can let Silence express itself. By marshaling such extraordinary daring to let go of everything that one holds onto and become empty, one opens oneself to ultimate life.

Centuries ago, Saint Dnyaneshwar demonstrated such a life for the masses. He received guidance from his brother Nivruttinath, so he could attain the state of Samadhi at such an early age. At the young age of twenty-one, he immersed himself and remained absorbed in the state of *Sanjeevan* Samadhi till the death of his physical body. Due to that grand feat, the world revers him and will continue to do so for ages to come.

The decision to give up his body while being absorbed in Silence, was possible only because of the conviction developed through continued practice of Silence for many years and the complete surrender of his body-mind.

In the same way, Jesus also immersed himself in the state of Silence while he was being crucified. This incident became instrumental for such a great cause. He was in the state of complete surrender when he gave up his body. He was firmly convinced, "Only Thy will can touch me." Despite the brutal torture of his physical body, Jesus exuded only forgiveness for those who committed the gruesome act. Thus, only divine will was being fulfilled through his body.

Let such a conviction arise within us too. Let this possibility unfold within us.

Questions for Contemplation

- What will you do to make meditation an integral part of your daily routine?

29

The Practice of Abiding in the Self

In the previous chapter, we learned about the states of Samadhi. Now, we are approaching the culmination of our journey of Silence. In this chapter, let us look at how we can dwell in Silence, even while we are actively engaged in the world. This is possible only when we develop uncompromising love and devotion towards the Self.

When we wake up, our behavioral patterns and tendencies drive us in the world. Our mind indulges in all sorts of sensory content. In deep sleep, all sensory distractions vanish, and we abide in Silence. When we wake up again, we forget our true nature and live the life of an individual. Thus, we remain bereft of the grand purpose for which we have received this body-mind.

Our mind perceives whatever it sees in the outside world as an object and assumes itself the seer of those objects. It also tries to apply this perspective to the experience of the Self. But the experience of the Self cannot be seen like we would see any other worldly object. It needs to be experienced differently. Our faith on the Guru, who imparts this training, helps us walk this path and make this experience possible.

Now, we will learn the art of de-focusing, with which we make the same world that was deluding us, instrumental for re-directing our attention to the Self. Let us understand this with some examples.

- There are cameras in which a small red bulb blinks just before shooting the picture. The bulb keeps blinking until the camera is focused and ready to take the picture. Imagine if such an arrangement were made to abide in the experience of the Self, how would life be?!

- Consider that you have been given a magnificent pair of glasses. When you wear the glasses and look at any object, a red pointer immediately starts blinking. Its blinking indicates, "Be in Silence." The red pointer keeps blinking as long as you focus on any object. As soon as you shift your focus inward and abide in Silence, it stops blinking. Thus, the blinking is an indication for you to be in Silence. If such glasses were made available, then one can easily become free from the illusory world!

Instead of waiting for such an invention, we can make such an arrangement for ourselves. As an experiment, imagine a red bulb blinking constantly when we look at anything in the world. The bulb keeps blinking on top of whatever we see, till we shift our focus to being in the Self.

For example, when we watch the TV, we will imagine the red bulb blinking there too. When we look at people, we will imagine a bulb blinking there too. It is indicating: "Be in the Self. Return to the experience of Silence." Till we return to the Self, the bulb will keep blinking.

And this is not just with external objects; we can imagine this with our thoughts too. With every thought that arises, we can picture the red bulb blinking at us. ....
....

It is as if every thought is actually telling us, "Why are you getting stuck in me? Be in the Self. Leave aside the temporary remedy; focus on the permanent solution." This will make it easier to be in the Self.

What does this really mean? If we see a mike in front of us, we say, "I saw a mike." But actually, we haven't seen the mike; we are seeing the Self. The mike is just a pretext, a mirror, that we use to experience the Self. When this happens consistently, then no weapons of the mind can affect us. We will begin to dip into Silence and dwell in the Self more often.

In this experiment, the red bulb represents the "witnessing of the world." There is no interest in witnessing the world. The real interest behind witnessing the world is to witness the Self. The world has been created so that it can be used as a pretext to know the Self.

Eyes cannot know themselves without any sight. Ears cannot know themselves without any sound. The nose cannot know its own presence without any smell. The skin knows itself only through the sensation of touch, and so it is with the tongue that needs taste to sense its own presence.

Similarly, imagine the Self as a grand cosmic eye, bigger than the world. When it sees the world, it experiences itself; the world is a mirror for the Self. The world comprises all sensations, emotions, and thoughts, which can be used to know the Self.

Whatever we look at, we will see the red bulb blinking in the middle. It will distract us from the scene. When we watch a movie on TV, we would have seen the news ticker or the stocks ticker scrolling at the bottom of the screen. We often find this ticker disturbing and want to get rid of it. The blinking red bulb is just like this ticker. It keeps blinking and the only way to get rid of it is to focus inward on Silence.

This exercise prepares us to dwell in Silence despite the tendencies of the body-mind. It makes it possible to be in Silence even whilst engaging in worldly activities. Here, using the word "despite" is important because it makes it easier to break our tendencies. We learn to de-focus from our tendencies and abide in Silence. Hence, we should practice this consistently.

This does not mean that we should ignore the happenings of the world. Of course, we will heed them and take necessary action. However, everything is an indication, an opportunity to shift to Silence.

Faith plays an important role in this consistent practice. With faith, we can turn every object, person, thought, emotion, ailment, or sensation into a blinking red pointer. We can take the support of whatever we perceive to practice being in Silence. The more we dwell in Silence, the more we begin to recognize it, and the more we love being in it!

Questions for Contemplation

- How will you remind yourself to practice the exercise given in this chapter during the entire day?

30

The Glory of Words Leading to Silence

On the final milestone of our journey of Silence, let us consider how words can help us return to Silence.

While engaging in the world, we use words for written and verbal communication. We gather information through the medium of words. There are several dictionaries that define the meanings of words. These words help us know more about the contents of the world.

But how would it be if we had a dictionary that helps us go beyond words into Silence? Such a dictionary is not available anywhere else. We need to create our own within ourselves.

The glory of words is indescribable! They can either entangle us in the contents of the illusory world or help us return to Silence. The Silence that pervades and transcends all words can be recognized and experienced through the medium of words themselves!

The purpose of words is to understand and make others understand. Words that don't serve this purpose cause noise. Words are like camels that help us cross the desert of ignorance. However, we should not forget our true nature after mounting the camel of words. Otherwise, they can entangle us in the wordy maze of worldly knowledge and bloat our ego. We deviate from the experience of the Self and live in the illusion of "I know."

Words that are backed by the wisdom and experience of Silence eradicate the noise within us and help us return to the Self. They are like the stick that holds the ice-cream of Silence. We need to hold the stick as long as we haven't experienced the coolness of ice-cream. Once we experience the coolness of Silence with the help of the stick of words, their purpose is served. We then need to throw away the stick of words. This coolness is helpful during the journey in the burning heat of the desert. It makes us alert and aware amidst the hot winds of the illusory world. Otherwise, if we keep chewing the stick of words without experiencing the coolness of Silence, words don't serve their purpose.

Now, we need to invest our energy in creating such a dictionary of words and thoughts that can lead us into Silence instead of investing it in words and thoughts that create noise. We need to inculcate such thoughts that can lead us into Silence, conserve and boost our energy, and awaken the latent power within us.

Self-realized saints have lived blissfully, being immersed in Silence. They used words for propagating their understanding to others. Left to themselves, they preferred to dwell in Silence. Listening to their words of wisdom shifts us from noise into Silence.

Both, the Self-realized Guru and other teachers, guide through the medium of words, but there is a difference between the two. Teachers use words to convey information; till the end we receive only words from whatever they convey.

On the other hand, words that are conveyed by a Self-realized Guru bear the essence of Silence within them. They eventually catapult the sincere seeker of Truth into Silence. The journey of these words leads to Silence! ....

....

The dictionary of words for Silence

When the mind is intoxicated with the topics of the world, it is not prepared to dip into Silence. At such times, we need to gain clarity about *why* we want to be in Silence.

When we patiently dwell in Silence, we begin to experience Silence by *being* Silence. The Self begins to experience itself. When Self-realization is attained through many more bodies, it is only then that the true purpose of creation of Earth will be fulfilled. Hence, the experience of Silence is of vital importance.

Until we are not clear about this purpose, we don't feel motivated about dwelling in Silence. Without clarity, being in Silence feels boring to the mind. Hence, we need to contemplate on the question: Why do I like Silence? This contemplation will propel us deep within into the experience of Silence.

Ask yourself, "I like Silence because…?" and see what answers emerge from within.

Some answers are given below—

…I like Silence because it is the experience of the true Self. It is the state of Self-realization. It is who I really am, my true nature. It is "nothing" that holds the potential of everything.

...I like Silence because I experience oneness with every being and feel sublime love while being in Silence.

...I like Silence because it can associate with all bodies, heal them, and express divine qualities through them.

...I like Silence because I *am* Silence.

...I like Silence because it remains untouched. It is indifferent to the changes in the world. I like freedom, and Silence is the ultimate freedom.

...I like Silence because it is Self-evident, Self-existing. It is its own cause. It is self-revealed.

...I like Silence because it awakens boundless power which helps in the highest creation.

...I like Silence because it has the potential to heal everyone. When we watch our body by being in Silence, its healing presence cures the body.

...I like Silence because it is transparent, crystal clear. Being in Silence, everything is seen with absolute clarity. That is the very purpose for which I (the Self) have associated with this body.

These are only some examples. You can compose such sentences from your heart for yourself, so that your mind gets motivated and won't make any excuses to avoid being in Silence.

These sentences serve the purpose of a dictionary of words that can help you return into Silence. When you use them, you will find yourself drawn into Silence even in the marketplace.

When you are in Silence, the Truth will become self-evident within, "I am that Silence which is present behind each word, behind every thought. I am that hidden nothingness, the zero that is not only present between two words but is present as the eternal backdrop of everything."

When this journey culminates, Silence alone prevails without any individual persona. The expression of divine qualities happens gracefully and harmoniously through the human harmonium!

Questions for Contemplation

- How committed do you find yourself to remember Silence at all times?
- Fill three answers:

    I like Silence because....

    I like Silence because....

    I like Silence because....

• • •

You can send your opinion or feedback on this book to:
Tej Gyan Foundation, P.O. Box 25, Pimpri Colony, Pimpri, Pune – 411017, Maharashtra, INDIA
Email: englishbooks@tejgyan.org

About Sirshree

Sirshree's spiritual quest, which began during his childhood, led him on a journey through various schools of thought and prevalent meditation practices. His overpowering desire to attain the Truth made him relinquish his teaching profession. After a long period of contemplation on the truth of life, his spiritual quest culminated in the attainment of the ultimate truth. Since then, over the last two decades, he has dedicated his life toward elevating mass consciousness and making spiritual pursuit simple and accessible to all.

Sirshree espouses, **"All paths that lead to the truth begin differently, but culminate at the same point – understanding. Understanding is complete in itself. Listening to this understanding is enough to attain the truth."**

Sirshree has delivered more than 3000 discourses that throw light on this understanding, simplify various aspects of life and unravel missing links in spirituality. He delivers the understanding in casual contemporary language by weaving profound aspects into analogies, parables and humor that provoke one to contemplate.

To make it possible for people from all walks of life to directly experience this understanding, Sirshree has designed the *Maha Aasmani Param Gyan Shivir* – a retreat designed as a comprehensive system for imparting wisdom. This system for wisdom, which has been accredited with ISO 9001:2015 certification, has inspired thousands of seekers from all walks of life to progress on their journey of the Truth. This system makes the wisdom accessible to every human being, regardless of religion, caste, social strata, country or belief system.

Sirshree is the founder of Tej Gyan Foundation, a no-profit organization committed to raising mass consciousness with branches in India, the United States, Europe and Asia-Pacific. Sirshree's retreats have transformed the lives of thousands and his teachings have inspired various social initiatives for raising global consciousness.

His published work includes more than 100 books, some of which have been translated in more than 10 languages and published by leading publishers. Sirshree's books provide profound and practical reading on existential subjects like emotional maturity, harmony in relationships, developing self-belief, overcoming stress and anxiety, and dealing with the question of life-beyond-death, to name a few. His literature on core spirituality expounds the deeper meaning of self-realization and self-stabilization, unravelling missing links in the understanding of karma, wisdom, devotion, meditation and consciousness.

Various luminaries and celebrities like His Holiness the Dalai Lama, publishers Mr. Reid Tracy, Ms. Tami Simon and Yoga Master Dr. B. K. S. Iyengar have released Sirshree's books and lauded his work. "The Source" book series, authored by Sirshree, has sold over 10 million copies in 5 years. His book, "The Warrior's Mirror", published by Penguin, was featured in the Limca Book of Records for being released on the same day in 11 languages.

Tejgyan... The Road Ahead
What is Tejgyan?

Tejgyan is the wisdom of the existential truth, which is beyond duality. "Gyan" is a term commonly used for "knowledge". Tejgyan is the wisdom beyond knowledge and ignorance. It is understanding that arises from direct experience of the final truth. It is what sets us free from the limitations of the mind and opens us to our highest potential.

In today's world, there are people who feel disharmony and are desperately trying to achieve balance in an unpredictable life. Tejgyan helps them in harmonizing with their true nature, the Self, thereby restoring balance in all aspects of their lives.

And then, there are those who are successful, but feel a sense of emptiness within. Tejgyan provides them fulfilment and helps them to embark on a journey towards self-realization. There are others who feel lost and are seeking the meaning of life. Tejgyan helps them to realize the true purpose of human life.

All this is possible with Tejgyan due to a very simple reason. The experience of the ultimate truth (God or Pure consciousness) is always available. The direct experience of this truth is possible provided the right method is known. Tejgyan is that method, that understanding.

The understanding of Tejgyan makes it possible to lead a life of freedom from fear, worry, anger and stress. It helps in attaining physical vitality, emotional strength and stability, harmony in relationships, financial freedom and spiritual progress.

At Tej Gyan Foundation, Sirshree imparts this understanding through a System for Wisdom – a series of retreats that guides participants step by step towards realizing the true Self, being established in the experience of self-realization, and expressing its qualities. This system for wisdom has been accredited with the ISO 9001:2015 certification.

Maha Aasmani Param Gyan Shivir

"**Maha Aasmani Param Gyan Shivir**" is the flagship Self-realization retreat offered by Tej Gyan Foundation. The retreat is conducted in Hindi. The teachings of the retreat are non-denominational (secular).

This residential retreat is held for 3 to 5 days at the foundation's MaNaN Ashram amidst the glory of the mountains and the pristine beauty of nature. The Ashram is located at the outskirts of the city of Pune in India, and is well connected by air, road and rail. The retreat is also held at other centres of Tej Gyan Foundation across the world.

You can participate in this retreat to attain ageless wisdom through a unique System for Wisdom so that you can:

1. Discover "Who am I" through direct experience.
2. Learn to abide in pure consciousness while functioning in the world, allowing the qualities of consciousness like peace, love, joy, compassion, abundance and creativity to manifest.
3. Acquire simple tools to use in everyday life, which help quiet the chattering mind.
4. Get practical techniques to be in the present and connect to the source of all answers within (the inner guru).
5. Discover missing links in the practices of Meditation (*Dhyana*), Action (*Karma*), Wisdom (*Gyana*) and Devotion (*Bhakti*).
6. Understand the nature of your body-mind mechanism to attain freedom form its tendencies.
7. Learn practical methods to shift from mind-centered living to consciousness-centered living.

A Mini-retreat is also conducted, especially for teenagers (14 to 16 years of age) during summer and winter vacations.

To register for retreats, visit www.tejgyan.org,

contact (+91) 9921008060, or email mail@tejgyan.com

About Tej Gyan Foundation

Tej Gyan Foundation (TGF) was established with the mission of creating a highly evolved society through all-round development of every individual that transforms all the facets of their lives. It is a non-profit organization, founded on the teachings of Sirshree.

The Foundation has received the ISO certification (ISO 9001:2015) for its system of imparting wisdom. It has centres all across India as well as in other countries. The motto of Tej Gyan Foundation is 'Happy Thoughts'.

At the core of the philosophy of Tejgyan is the Power of Acceptance. Acceptance has profound meaning and is at the core of our Being. It is Acceptance that brings forth true love, joy and peace.

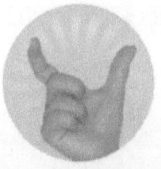

Symbol of Acceptance

The Symbol of Acceptance – shown above – is a representation of this truth. The symbol represents brackets. Whatever occurs in life falls within these brackets that signify acceptance of whatever is. Hence, this symbol forms the centerpiece of the Foundation's MaNaN Ashram.

The Foundation is creating a highly evolved society through:
- Tejgyan Programs (Retreats, YouTube Webcasts)
- Tejgyan Books and Apps
- Tejgyan Projects (Value education, Women empowerment, Peace initiatives)

The Foundation undertakes projects to elevate the level of consciousness among students, youth, women, senior citizens, teachers, doctors, leaders, professionals, corporate and Government organizations, police force, prisoners etc.

Good News!

Maha Aasmani Param Gyan Retreat
is now conducted ONLINE in Hindi!

You can participate in the retreat from the convenience of your home. The retreat is conducted in 3 parts during weekends:

1. The Foundation Truth retreat

2. The Bright Responsibility retreat

3. The Maha Aasmani final retreat

For more details, please call: +91 9921008060, +91 9921008075

To register, visit: https://www.tejgyanglobal.org/mareg

Books can be delivered at your doorstep by registered post or courier. You can request the same through postal money order or pay by VPP. Please send the money order to either of the following two addresses:

WOW Publishings Pvt. Ltd.

1. Registered Office: E-4, Vaibhav Nagar, Near Tapovan Mandir, Pimpri, Pune - 411017.

2. Post Box No. 36, Pimpri Colony Post Office, Pimpri, Pune - 411017

Phone No: (+91) 9011013210 / 9623457873

You can also order your copy at the online store:

www.gethappythoughts.org

*Free Shipping plus 10% Discount on purchases above Rs. 500/-

SELECT BOOKS AUTHORED BY SIRSHREE

   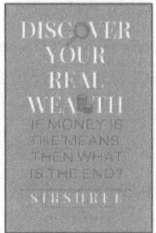

To order these and other books authored by Sirshree
Visit **www.gethappythoughts.org**

For further details contact:
Tejgyan Global Foundation
Registered Office:
Happy Thoughts Building, Vikrant Complex, Near Tapovan Mandir, Pimpri, Pune 411017, Maharashtra, India.
Contact No: 020-27411240, 27412576
Email: mail@tejgyan.com

MaNaN Ashram:
Survey No. 43, Sanas Nagar, Nandoshi gaon, Kirkatwadi Phata, Sinhagad Road, Tal. Haveli, Dist. Pune 411024, Maharashtra, India.
Contact No: 992100 8060.
Hyderabad: 9885558100, Bangalore: 9880412588,
Delhi : 9891059875, Nashik: 9326967980, Mumbai: 9373440985

For accessing our unique 'System for Wisdom' from self-help to self-realization, please follow us on:

	Website Online Shopping/ Blog	www.tejgyan.org www.gethappythoughts.org
twitter	Video Channel	www.youtube.com/tejgyan For Q&A videos: http://goo.gl/YA81DQ
facebook	Social networking	www.facebook.com/tejgyan
twitter	Social networking	www.twitter.com/sirshree
	Internet Radio	http://www.tejgyan.org/internetradio.aspx

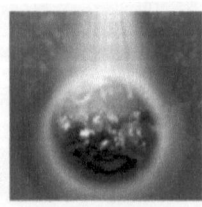

Pray for World Peace along with thousands of others every day at 09:09am and 09:09pm

Divine Light of Love, Bliss and Peace is Showering;
The Golden Light of Higher Consciousness is Rising;
All negativity on Earth is Dissolving;
Everyone is in Peace and Blissfully Shining;
O God, Gratitude for Everything!

www.ingramcontent.com/pod-product-compliance
Lightning Source LLC
LaVergne TN
LVHW041221080526
838199LV00082B/1349